Just Keep Going North...

You'll Know When You Get There!

Breath-Taking, Unforgivable
Short & Tall Stories
About Duluth &
The Head-O-The Lakes.

Just Keep Going North...

You'll Know When You Get There!

Breath-Taking, Unforgivable
Short & Tall Stories
About Duluth &
The Head-O-The Lakes.

Art Director
Jeff S. Sonstegard

Design/Computer Layout
Allen E. Holappa
Jeff C. Knobbe

Copyright ©1991 by Rick Eichert
First published in 1992 by
Sterling Design & Publishing, Inc.

Library of Congress Catalog Card Number:
92-080568
ISBN 0-9630328-3-6

All rights reserved. No part of this publication be reproduced or used in any form or by any means—graphic, electronic, or mechanical, including photocopying, recording, taping, or information storage and retrieval systems— without written permission of the publisher.

First printing, 1992
1 2 3 4 5 6 7 8 9

TABLE OF CONTENTS

PROLOGUE

1. WELL, FOR STARTERS...   4

2. BEING IN THE RIGHT SPOT...   7

3. THE SNOW-BIRDS ARE BACK...   23

4. SURE ARE A LOT OF SMART CATS...   26

5. GUESS WHO I AM & WHAT I DO...   30

6. IF SUMMER ARRIVES THIS YEAR...   39

7. WATER'S NOT SUPPOSED TO HAVE ...   49

8. THE PERSONALIZED FAST-TRACK SAUNA &...   54

9. IT COULD HAPPEN...   58

10. NOW, ISN'T THAT REALLY SOMETHING...   61

11. HOW ABOUT SOME FREE ADVICE FOR...   76

12. MOST PEOPLE WON'T EVEN KNOW THE...   82

13. IT'S THE SAME EVERY FALL...   90

14. LIFE'S LITTLE STUMBLING BLOCKS...   93

15. WHAT'S THERE TO SAY...   101

16. NOW THAT'S A REAL PARADE...   106

This book is mostly a work of fiction. Names, characters, places, and incidents are either the product of the author's imagination or are used fictitiously. Any resemblance to actual events or locales, or persons, living or dead, is intirely coincidental.3

PROLOGUE

RICK EICHERT

Obliquely, but of course with a degree of curious good taste, I've been asked why anyone would write such downright trivial stories, almost malicious in intent, about the City and good people of Duluth. Was this an exercise in free speech? Did I have some grudge? Was I suffering from some undiagnosed character disorder ... year-round cabin fever, maybe even cultural deprivation or anomie? It beats me.

It seems the answer is much more obvious: if a person spends close to forty years in Duluth, something has to give. So, the pressure just got to me and I got to a word processor and, the next thing you know, here are all these improbable stories pouring out. Naturally, these stories take some explaining.

For example: some people don't know where Duluth is and could probably care less, so I'm not going to tell them right away. Actually, Duluth is more like a state of mind than a real place. But, unfortunately, only a few people, called Duluthians, truly have this state of mind in place. True, a few well-meaning geographers insist that Duluth is located at the end of Lake Superior. It was a choice of either putting Duluth there or labeling the entire area as "Mostly Unexplored Territory," periodically claimed by Minnesota.

Any tourist over the past twenty-five years could tell you that where they've been up north, at the Head-O-The-Lakes, that couldn't really be Duluth. No way! It doesn't at all resemble the pictures in the tourist promotional brochures. For starters, where's the sun? Why aren't people swimming in Lake Superior, like the pictures show? Where are all the fun places? How come you have to learn about the cold, the fog, and the bugs in July firsthand, not from the Tourist Bureau?

So, don't confuse Duluth with a place, because it isn't exactly that. Duluth is more like things that happen to you when you lose control and someone then asks you: "So whad'ja learn from that experience?"

On the other hand, though, Duluth is so much on the move, at least if you ask city politicians and developers, it's hard to know

Just Keep Going North..

where Duluth really is. At times it seems to be someplace back in yesteryear, while at other times it's that vague promise of a tomorrow. It's never actually anything special, never smallest or biggest, never first or greatest. Yet, unlike many fictional towns in Minnesota, which must remain nameless, it's neither mediocre nor just a little bit better than average. Those kinds of ratings and rankings don't mean much to Duluthians, who have come to appreciate being in-between.

After all, being a Duluthian has no value unless it's zealously practiced, along with a select number of other virtues. And, fortunately, Duluthians have a whole range of virtues — from sullen stubbornness to unbeatable dourness. How many other cities could claim such wide-ranging, distinctive competencies, not to mention world-class industrialists, plus a pretty fair chunk of lakeshore? But, then, how many cities could drop from a population of 125,000 to 85,000 with such dignity and grace?

These stories are really an effort to pinpoint where Duluth is, how it got there, but not why, just in case anybody is looking for it. Or, if they should discover it by accident, it will help them to survive until help arrives.

The Duluth Tourist Bureau has been running a campaign for years, called Discover Duluth. So, gentle reader, here's your chance to win overnight fame by "discovering Duluth" in these pages. It's gotta' be in here somewhere.

Of course, all of the events portrayed in these stories are true, because I say they are, and no other city apparently wants to claim them. If you doubt their authenticity, you probably applaud politicians when they say, "For more taxes." True, healthy skepticism is what the reader/explorer needs when venturing into this territory, with camera, kids, and camper. The real point is: if these things haven't happened in Duluth exactly as I've told them, you can be sure they will pretty soon (there's something to be said for that kind of truth, too). That's how things happen in Duluth. Like the stone skipping contest. That's about to be true, but it's scheduled for next year, along with the escalator for fish out in Lester River, right by the mouth of the river in the park, about a quarter mile up.

So, while you're waiting for the fog to clear, if you want a guaranteed adventure that's better than a live Northland vacation, start reading. I recommend you read the book before you come to

Just Keep Going North..

Duluth, if that thought has remotely crossed your mind; to do it the other way around would take all the fun out of looking for familiar landmarks and people and, especially, their foibles. And, believe me, there are still foibles in Duluth; the local wild ones are so much better than those store-bought kinds shipped in from the Twin Cities.

Gathering foibles in Duluth doesn't require a license at present, but I understand the City Council is considering such a move, as the folks who run the bed and board places relate it. So, if you read fast, you can find out where to get the really great foibles. Hmmmm, are they ever tasty!

Last, some stories about Duluth require only a minimum telling, an almost unfinished quality. Some stories might seduce readers out on thin ice, with a resulting ankle-deep plunge into Duluth life and culture. Unfortunately, other stories involve details and development that plummet the reader into a web of characters, values, and unlikely events. There's no middle ground, gentler or firmer. Then, too, you will simply have to put up with the writing style, the abundant use of commas for breathing points, semicolons to handle thought-tangents, and the random design of paragraphs as the standard regional idiom ... or something like that, if you want to read something important and good into these stories.

RICK EICHERT,

    Somewhere in Uncharted N.E. Minnesota, close by Lake Superior.

    January 1992,

Chapter one

Well, For Starters

In general, it's safest to begin with simple stories about Duluthians. Things will get complicated fast enough without overdoing it, which is what Duluthians like best.

For starters, most Duluthians have two names: an "out-there" name and a "go-by" name. Teachers, doctors, and the people over at the banks tend to use a person's out-there name, while co-workers, barbers, and service station operators and the like use a person's go-by name.

Nearly every native Duluthian sooner or later gets a go-by name; newcomers, however, are just called newcomers until they leave. They have to use an out-there name, whether it's Winthrop, Vivian, Gerald, or Francis; it can never become Win, Viv, Gerry, or Frank or some outlandish nickname, because nicknames aren't the same as go-by names. True, some Duluthians have nicknames for use in places like Superior, Minneapolis, or over at the Brainerd racetrack, but nicknames don't have much currency in Duluth. A newcomer once tried to get his co-workers to use his nickname, which was Bic, but they pretty much stayed with Bickford or pretended he didn't have a name at all. Names are fairly serious business around here.

It seems that Duluthians are blessed with a rich ethnic heritage, and that ethnic heritage is portioned out when a person can least cope with it, at birth or when he or she is baptized. It's not uncommon for a person to wind up with a name like Gustav Jurgens Thorstenson, or Gottfried Helmuth Krumschroder, or Magda Linnea Lundwald, or even Helga Ingebord Peterson. Naturally, in giving these names to infants as a means for honoring grandparents, aunts, and uncles, it goes without saying that something good has to come out of all this naming business. So the child gets an official out-there name, and it's on the records forever.

(This past week brought a major event to the Oskar K. (K. stands for Knute) Fryklund family. A boy was born after a string of daughters ranging from five to sixteen years in age. The arrival of that boy, the heir presumptive to the family-owned laundry business, was of more than whispered relief down at Gloria Dei Lutheran

Just Keep Going North..

Church, down on 6th Avenue East and 3rd Street, because it meant that, perhaps, just perhaps, the Norwegian church wouldn't be closed or consolidated with the Swedish congregation at First Lutheran (Old Elim Lutheran Church), down on Superior Street. Now there was one more member. And, in such a declining area, every newly christened child keeps things going. (The last baptism down at Gloria Dei was two years ago.) So, baptized he was, and he was christened Oskar Tingwald Fryklund but given the go-by name of Ting.)

It helps to have a go-by name. If someone asks, "Hey, dude, what'cha go by?", the person doesn't have to say: "My name is Oskar Tingwald Fryklund." Or, in job hunting or in talking to the Reserve Sergeant, the person doesn't have to repeat something like Oskar T. Fryklund, while the listener tries to figure out whether the speaker is pulling his leg, speaking Danish, or has a mild speech defect. The person can just say quite normally, "My name's Ting Fryklund, OK, you got it? There it is. It's Ting. Wanna' repeat it once or twice for practice?"

Sometimes, before the christening ceremony, the parents let the godparents know what the family has picked out for the child's go-by name. And, you can be sure the godparents will say something like, "Oh, 'fer sure, he looks just like a Ting," or that girl is sure a little Peep, or she's just like Aunt Bette, and that's how the go-by name gets stuck on. At other times, the go-by name gets there under its own power. However it gets there, once the go-by name is decided on, everybody can pretty much forget about the out-there name, except the relative whose name is guaranteed one more generation of use.

Many brides have been surprised at their weddings when the minister turned to the groom and said, "Do you, Hjalmer Olaf Lyngblad, take this woman for your lawfully wedded wife?" The bride, in turn, looks at her future spouse and says, "I thought your name was Ole ... what's this Hjalmer stuff? Does that mean I've gotta' use that name out there? ... Wait a minute, I've got some second thoughts about this deal!"

Then, too, there have been some episodes in Duluth when the go-by names haven't been so good. In one case, a relative into his cups after the christening noticed that the infant had extremely small ears, the child's christening cap having almost hidden the fact. The inebriated relative made the off-handed comment to his wife that he

Just Keep Going North..

hoped the child had good eyes, because they were never going to able to put spectacles on that one. And, because another relative overheard that remark, the child went through life being called Specs. It's probably no worse than the middle-aged woman with the go-by name of Oopsie, the utterance the minister made when he dropped the baptism manual into the font. It seems that name stuck like glue. Yep, Oopsie Maki made the most of that go-by name, which is more than can be said for most people with conventional names such as Beth, Rudy, or Bob.

So, in proper Duluth society at least, if you hear some unusual names, names that sound as if they might be Scandinavian mixed with Italian, or a Polish word with a Spanish sound to it, be assured that none of these ethnic groups are involved in assigning go-by names. Trixie, Mookie, Chooch, Ding, Bubsy, Crank, Floss, and Wyo are just go-by names and let it go at that. But feel free to call people by their go-by name in Duluth, because that's what people expect.

Chapter two

Being In The Right Spot At The Right Time

John Halverson wasn't one of those people who let winter creep up on him by pretending that fall might last more than three weeks to a month. He was ready for it. He started getting ready about mid-August, so he had a lot of extra time on his hands. And, being retired gave him a lot more time than he'd ever imagined and far more than his wife, Marion, could bear.

It had gotten to the point where Marion started to make up jobs for JoJo (his endearment name), like counting clothes pins and jam or jelly glasses, sorting out old decks of cards, even packaging up their penny collection in the fifty-cent coin wrappers she'd gotten from the bank, but naturally only after each penny was checked for possible coin-collector value. Marion started making up errands just to get John out of the house for awhile. She'd send him over to the hardware store for shelving paper, and he'd be gone for forty-five minutes, which was just how much time she needed to run a load of clothes through the wash. She'd send him over to First Bank to deposit their retirement checks, which gave her enough time to make a few phone calls in relative privacy.

All in all, it was getting somewhat unbearable, the way John followed her from task to task, from room to room, asking if there was anything he could do. It might have been a bit different if John were of an amorous bent, if he were following Marion around in order to rekindle that old flame. But, after four children, and some forty-one years of marriage, Marion knew the kindling was still there, but maybe John forgot where he put the matches, so to speak. So, with a clear conscience, she kept him as busy as possible at just plain busy work.

Marion finally suggested that John and his friends, well, maybe, they might want to consider getting some fishing in. This time she really planted the right idea. But, then, John always had some excuse, like maybe he should take the car in for a winter tune-up, or maybe he should drive over and see Shirley, his favorite daughter-in-law, or maybe he ought to send Kevin (he's their oldest son) that old 20-gauge shotgun up in the attic. He didn't know for sure, but there were a lot of things that he could do. But, John was more used

Just Keep Going North..

to taking directions, rather than getting his own starter going, if what the neighbors say is true.

John did have one modest hobby. He enjoyed lake trout fishing. He used to go fishing with Al Olsen, Elmer Davidson, and Einer ("Hjenje") Sorenson. Those were good times, especially if they took out Olsen's boat and trolled along the North Shore. But Elmer was getting more and more crippled up with arthritis and he didn't get around much. And, old man Sorenson, he spent most of his time down at that senior citizen place, trying to cozy up to that Millie Hagen. John himself didn't go in for that sort of stuff, but then Hjenje's wife, Lucille, had been dead these past seven years.

Nowadays, John pretty much fished when he could on shore, up on Stoney Point, a few miles past the French River, where Davidson liked to go. But Davidson was recuperating from some sort of heart surgery and his wife didn't want him sitting out there in the cold weather. Still, John liked fishing. He even caught a few, when he was at the right spot. Yep, John knew the right spot on Stoney Point and he thought of it as his spot. It was right at the end of the Stoney Point Road, just where those two huge boulders divide and a rock ledge extends out into the lake. That ledge could be slippery when the waves wet the algae. But when the water was calm, a person could cast out maybe thirty or forty feet, right where those trout liked to feed.

John didn't have that much when it came to fishing gear and tackle, but then what he had was all right by him. After thirty-six years with the DM & N, a man didn't need very much. He had a decent pension, and at his age the thought of buying a new fishing pole, why, that was downright wasteful. But, then, it was wasteful not to use the fishing poles he had, too. The more he thought about it, the more he thought that right there in the basement, right there where it sat since his last fishing trip some three years back, was that fishing pole doing nothing but getting a bit dusty, and the reel probably needed some oiling. Yep, those were the thoughts that held his attention as he brought in the last peck of Evinrude Early Start/Late Ending cucumbers that Marion had asked him to harvest. Yep, it's a waste to have those fishing poles just sitting there. Maybe he could send one to David (his second son), but what would an insurance adjuster in Keokuk, Iowa, do with a fishing pole? Besides, David didn't like fishing.

8

Just Keep Going North..

He remembered taking David fishing up on the Baptism River, when David was nine. Yep, it was on the east branch of the Baptism, just east of Vinland, Minnesota. Stupid kid, mused John, he musta' stared into the water so long, he got hypnotized or something and just plain fell into the river. Spoiled the whole trip; David never did catch a fish and, curiously, never did get into fishing after that more than he had to.

John thought that maybe he'd call up Al Olsen and see if he wanted to go fishing. He'd tell Al it was a shame to keep those fishing poles around just to look at. Maybe he could even talk old man Davidson's wife into letting Elmer out for an afternoon, just up to Stoney Point. Well, it was worth thinking about.

By the middle of the second week of September, John had done a lot of thinking. At seventy-three, it's not thinking that's difficult. In fact, it's easier in a way; it's taking action that's hard. It was easy to visualize being out there on Stoney Point; he'd even driven up the North Shore and down Stoney Point Road last Sunday. He took Marion and one of the grandchildren along. They'd stopped right there on the northern end of Stoney Point Road, and John showed Marion where his favorite fishing spot was, as if she was hearing it for the first time.

"Yep, right there, right between those two boulders, where the ledge sticks out in the water a bit. Caught an eight pounder, a real nice one. It was a struggle and I almost lost it. Good thing Al had the net ready. Boy, that was some fishing."

"Did'ja hear that, Bobby?" he asked his grandchild.

"Bobby, Robert, did you hear what Grandpa said?" said Marion.

"Yes, Grandma, he's only told me it about a hundred times, like every time we come out here. When are you goin' to take me fishing, like you did with my dad, Grandpa?"

So, September wasn't getting any younger and neither was John Halverson. On Sunday last, he called up Al Olsen and discussed the chances of making one last fishing trip for the season up on Stoney Point. Yes, Wednesday would be a good day, so would Thursday next, hell, almost any day, even Saturday, would be fine. Al said he'd think about it and get back to him on Tuesday.

Just Keep Going North..

Later at Tara's Store, John learned that Hjenje Sorenson had a heart attack, right down at the senior citizen's center, playing bingo with Millie Hagen. It seems Millie won about $150 and Hjenje got a bit too excited. And, now he was down at one of those expensive care units, as the Seniors describe it.

"Well, no point in calling old man Sorenson at this time," said John, as he shared this unfortunate news with Marion.

"Well, JoJo, that's too bad about Sorenson," said Marion. "Stop down and see him maybe on Monday. I hear that Millie Hagen really had a crush on 'Hjenje-Boy,' as she called him. I'll bet she's feelin' pretty bad. That's her third boyfriend in less than two years ... and, you know that Millie Hagen is quite the get-about these days, though I heard she's not driving anymore.

"Did you hear 'bout that accident she got into, down there on 1st Street? Oh, she was pulling out from in front of Metzger's Meats — you know where I mean — with no turn signals on, and this real distinguished gent comes around the corner on 1st Street and 2nd Avenue, and the next thing you know, she gets distracted and hits this Northland Electric Company truck. Trudy Jacobsen was with her and you know how Trudy is. She told everybody about it over at church, like Sadie and Tizz. So, I want you to be real careful driving on 1st Street. You never know when a truck will come barrelling out of nowhere ... and with those bricks in the street, you can't stop like you used to, 'cause the surface is so slippery.'

"JoJo, why don't you call Elmer's wife and see if he could go out with you. If you park the car close by the shore, he could sit in there if he got cold," suggested Marion.

"Oh, I don't know. It's so hard talking to Lee. She's, oh, you know what I mean. These days she's just like a mother hen, since Elmer got that whatcha-ma-call-it installed to regulate his heart. She won't even let him get near their microwave, for fear it'll upset that contraption. Maybe you could call and ask her for me. We just want to be out for a few hours."

Well, Marion did call and the answer was still no. Lee Davidson was sure that Elmer's doctor didn't want him sitting outside that long and, besides, if he caught a fish, it could put too great a strain on him. Those were her thoughts on the matter and that was it.

Just Keep Going North..

* * *

Well, that fishing trip got put together finally. John convinced Al Olsen and his friend, Ryner ("Pete") Peterson that some shoreline fishing would be all right. He promised to take his grandson, Bobby, along, too. John explained to Al and Pete that Bobby was a good kid. If he got out of hand, he'd just have to sit in the car. Pete and Al agreed; it was OK to take a kid fishing, if he didn't get in the way too much.

It took the better part of Thursday morning to get everything assembled. There was the trip over to Pete's house on 9th Street, the trip over to Al's house on Snelling Avenue, and then he picked up Bobby on Lakeview Drive. They had along a Coleman ice chest with food and a few beers and pop, plus a thermos of coffee. There were those big five-level tackle boxes, fishing poles, nets, stringers, extra jackets, caps, folding chairs, rain gear, and Lord knows what else that was put carefully into John's Chevy trunk. With places appropriately assigned in the car, the fishing expedition began.

That is, until John remembered he'd forgotten to get a few minnows. Minnows are like teasers for trout. They add to the overall bait appeal in a way that an artificial lure could never do alone. They'd have to head over to the Sportsman Center, over there on 57th Avenue East, and get a few minnows. It wouldn't be real lake trout fishing without minnows.

At the Sportsman Center, the trade was pretty thin. Only one helper and the owner were on duty since the season was coming to an end. But there were three other customers and they caught John's eye. They looked like trout fisherman, the kind that liked to fish from shore.

"Where you guys goin' fishing?" inquired John, while admonishing Bobby to keep his hands out of the minnow tanks.

"Oh, we heard about this place up the North Shore, Stormy Point or Stoney Point, is the place to go," said the taller of the three men. "I heard that's really good fishing this time of year. One of my friends, down in Dubuque, said he'd caught three good-size lake trout at that place, right where a ledge sticks out over the lake. Ever been there? Had any luck there?"

Just Keep Going North..

John sized these fishermen up and down slowly. Of course he'd heard of it. It was called Stoney Point ... it was where he and his buddies fished. It was *their* spot.

"Oh, yeah, everybody knows about Stoney Point, but I heard the fishing's not that good there any more. Used to be a good place, but hardly anybody fishes there anymore. Mostly, the waves are too high ... can't cast out far enough ... easy to lose a lure and about fifty feet of line on those rocks down there. Were you folks goin' up there?" John asked cautiously.

"Well, we hadn't made up our minds yet," said one of the strangers. "We were just thinking about checking matters out. Maybe, unless there's something else you'd recommend."

"Oh, I always tell people about the mouth of the Talmadge or up at Gooseberry Falls. Those are both real good places, with a lotta' coho in there," suggested John.

"Let's go. I wanta' get out fishin'" blurted out Bobbie, as he pulled his grandpa's arm. "C'mon, Gramps, let's go. You promised to show me how to catch fish."

As they left the Sportsman Center, John noticed that the only non-Minnesotan plates in the parking lot were from Iowa. Yep, he thought, those Iowans sure are fast learners. Pretty soon they'd know every good fishing spot in Minnesota, and that'd happen before Minnesota could start limiting the number of out-of-state fishing licenses. Those "outa-state types" were sure taking over all of the good fishing spots.

After making one more stop so Al could relieve himself on the Congdon Boulevard park area, the group headed for Stoney Point. They took the scenic route, the one that clings to the shoreline, and then followed the dirt road to Stoney Point. There was only one other car there. It had Iowa plates.

On the roadway, John began his "fishin'" lecture to Bobby, as they took the gear out of the trunk. "Well, now, Bobby, you listen to me and you might even catch a fish, a lake trout so big it'd take all four of us to get it in," said John. "Yep, you just pay attention to what I do and you do the same thing. Now for starters, hold the reel like this and put your left hand here ...." John droned on to Bobby about how to do what every Duluth kid almost knows intuitively. "Now, do it right, pay attention ... and listen to what I say, 'cause that's what matters most," concluded John.

Bobby heard what he wanted to hear, which wasn't much. (But, if any lake trout had been listening, they could have learned more about themselves than they'd probably want to know, and from a trout fisherman, too. Those fish might have re-examined their entire role in this matter, had they known what John expected of them.)

As the party walked down the trail to the shoreline, John's hidden fear was confirmed. Doggone it all! Those Iowans got there first. You bet they had. Those three Iowans were standing right there on the rock ledge, the one that extends a bit over the lake. They were quietly reeling in their lines, re-casting, and otherwise acting as if they owned the place. They were right where John wanted to fish. They had the *best* spot, right where the ledge jutted into the lake, with deep pools below them; places where the lake trout swarmed and held sway, places where shadows blended with the rippled surface, deep in the waters where algae-covered boulders hid insects and crawdads. The water flickered with tiny minnows.

"We shoulda' got here sooner ... I shoulda' told Al to hold it until we got here," muttered John to himself. He was upset; he was angry that he'd not been able to convince these Iowans to go elsewhere; he was convinced these Iowans weren't going to leave this place — his spot — without some real prodding.

"If it's OK with you guys, we'll just fish over here," suggested Pete Peterson, as he set down his tackle box and gear as close to the ledge as fishing courtesy allowed. "We'll just cast a bit to the west," he added.

Horse-apples, thought John, a word he'd learned from re-runs of "*M.A.S.H.*" but one he never used in public. If we're goin' catch any fish, we need that spot. Can't catch any fish side-casting from the edges ... gotta' get right out there on the ledge and see what happens.

An Iowan caught a lake trout. It was a beauty, close to nine pounds, everyone agreed.

"How'd ya figure out how much that fish weighed?" asked Bobby, adding, "Whad'ja do, just guess together?" Bobby's sense of humor was on target, since fisher folk have a tendency to underestimate on the positive side if from Duluth.

"Hey, kid, what's your name? Bobby? OK. You come over here and take my place for awhile," shouted one of the Iowans. "I'd like to see you catch a fish. Been fishin' long?" he asked.

Just Keep Going North..

"Naw, I only get to fish, maybe a coupl'a times a year. My dad likes fishin' OK, but he doesn't have time these days. Isn't it great? I'm fishin' with my Grampa. He's a real good fisherman, like Superman, and he gets all the trout."

Bobby's comments creased smile lines in Al's face. He knew when John had caught fish, how, and where. Hearing Bobby's praise for John, Pete just nodded and snickered.

The fishing wasn't going well at all. There'd been no strikes, no signs of trout, no action whatsoever for more than forty minutes. The sun repeatedly tried to thrust its rays between low-hanging morning clouds, as the cloud bank layered deeper and deeper over Stoney Point. To the south, mantles of gray-blue clouds swept earthward, blending with the barely discernible Wisconsin shore. The wind began to toss the lingering yellow birch leaves, their rustling adding to the cry of a solitary crow. This was shoreline trout fishing at its best.

The mid-morning wind picked up and began to counter-riffle the shallow waves along the shoreline, as packets of wind broke through the tree cover.

It was still except for the occasional sound of a reel and the splash of the lure. Pete Peterson sat in a lawn chair, his coffee cup half full, as he was prone to comment. "Yep," he said, "time to get a refill. What kinda' coffee is this? Is this ARCO or one of those fancy brands?" he jokingly asked John.

"Naw, that's just what the wife's been making for years. She gets one of those big cans of coffee on sale and mixes it with one of those expensive kinds. Can't tell the difference, she says, but then it takes some gettin' used to, since you never know what brand it is. S'ppose it doesn't matter, 'cept when she has her lady friends over for a luncheon. Yep, those ladies over at our church have been trying to match Marion's coffee for years, but she won't tell them her secret."

"I'm hungry, Gramps, can I have a sandwich?" asked Bobby.

"Sure," replied John, "just put the lid back on the cooler. We wouldn't want anything to get too warm out here or draw any bears." With the morning temperature about forty-five degrees, this sort of humor didn't even get any response from Al. But mention of bears made Bobby's eyes widen.

Just Keep Going North..

"There ain't no bears out here, are there, Gramps? I mean they're in the woods, but they wouldn't come down here, would they?" asked Bobby.

"One time I was here," interjected Al, "and I seen a brown bear and two cubs right over there by the road, right by that trash barrel up there. That bear had garbage all over the place. 'Course, when we got outa' the car, those cubs scampered like they'd seen a ghost. But that mother bear just stood there and then dragged a whole bag of garbage with her back into the woods."

"Wow! That's cool," said Bobby. "I wonder if they're still around?"

Pete couldn't help but get in his two cents. "Hey, Bobby, what Mr. Olsen means is that he saw three raccoons. Mr. Olsen has a tendency to exaggerate a bit because his memory plays tricks on him. The only place he ever saw a bear was out at the zoo." Pete laughed and so did John: Bobby didn't know what to believe.

"No, no, it's the truth," protested Al. "Those bears weren't no raccoons. They were real bears and my memory reminds me that you still owe me $25 for those Shriner Circus tickets."

The banter continued, with Al barely matching Pete for teasing. Of course, with Bobby there, these old gents didn't make anything too explicit.

The morning wore on. At around eleven, a second Iowan landed a lake trout. A bit smaller than the first one, but certainly a "keeper."

"Man, look at that fish," said Bobby. "That's a beaut. When are we goin' to get one, Gramps?"

John's face tightened. He'd get a fish if those Iowans weren't in *his* spot. He'd show Bobby, and even Al, what real trout fishing was all about. But it didn't seem as if those Iowans were going to move.

"Going to fish all day?" posed John to the Iowans, "or are you heading back to tall corn country later on?" He thought if he could remind those Iowans of how far away they were from home, how difficult the traffic was going through the Twin Cities, even the possibility of a surprise snowfall, maybe they'd leave. Maybe he'd even tell them about a couple of other spots that were better. Maybe, he could tell them the DNR regularly checked Stoney Point for

Just Keep Going North..

out-state fishermen to see if they had the proper trout stamps, because a lot of these out-staters didn't know about fishing rules.

"Aren't those new trout stamps colorful," said John to nobody in particular, adding, "you'd think everybody would want to have a set. I heard tell some folks from Nebraska were fishing out here last year, and they didn't know about trout stamps. Guess it cost them a pretty penny and a lotta time explaining to those DNR game wardens what they were doing with four lake trout and no trout stamps. 'Course, we older guys get a break on those stamps. I suppose you guys from Iowa hadda' pay full price, right?" asked John.

"Oh, sure, I got about sixteen years of trout stamps. I save 'em and give 'em to my friends," remarked one of the Iowans, a bit annoyed by John's curious remark.

Noon came a bit late, and was determined more by mild pangs of hunger than the clock. The men and the boy huddled behind the rock ledge and ate the sturdy sandwiches Marion had made.

"You can't beat Marion's egg-salad sandwiches," said Al. "I bet she makes the best when it comes to egg salad." Bobby didn't think so; he liked his grandma's peanut butter and marmalade best. No, Bobby didn't want any sardines, as the men passed around the tin. He'd pass on the pickled beets, too.

"How come you eat that stuff, Grandpa? Does Grandma make you do it?" he asked.

"Now, watch your manners there," said John. "Your grandma is a very good cook and if you don't like her cooking, well, I'm certain Al or me could just eat your portion of this apple pie and easily finish off these cookies here, too. But then, you might still be a bit hungry."

Bobby knew his grandpa was kidding him; his grandpa's eyes squinted when he was trying to be funny. "I love you, Gramps," he said, "even if you do eat kinda' funny food." John pushed him good-naturedly and Bobby rolled over, pretending to be hurt.

"Let's get back to fishing," suggested Pete. It was cooling down; the wind had increased somewhat and a flock of gulls had moved into the bay east of Stoney Point.

* * *

Al had something. His line suddenly snapped up. His reel whizzed nylon line forward until he brought his finger slowly across the release.

"I think I got one," whispered Al. The line was moving clearly eastward through the water and then sharply plunged, causing the reel to whistle more line out. "It's going down," muttered Al, "I gotta' keep it away from those boulders down there. Got that net handy?" he asked.

That fish and Al played a back and forth game for close to five minutes. Al tried to reel in, but then that fish would run deep. Al was starting to sweat. The veins on his face stood out. This was exciting. Even Bobby reeled in fast so he could watch the whole affair.

"What's it feel like? How big is it, Mr. Olsen? What's it doing now?" asked Bobby. "Geez, I wish I was that lucky."

It was a toss-up as to who was getting more tired: the fish or Al Olsen. This wasn't like watching fishing on TV. This was work. Al kept his eyes on the line, trying to get that fish closer and closer to shore. He walked from his casting spot to the elevated rocky edge of the lake. Both John and Pete held their nets at ready, allowing Al plenty of room to get that fish up to shore. The fish briefly broke the surface about fifteen feet from shore and then plunged. As the fish surfaced, Al got a cramp in his leg. (He was getting these cramps more often and they were pretty painful.)

"Oh, oh, ohhwww," moaned Al. "I got a cramp in my leg. It's killing me. I don't think I can land it. Ohh, it's awful! I gotta' sit down." And, as he agonizingly tried to sit down, there was a slackening in the line. The line went limp. The fish was free, off the hook. Gone.

"Well, we'll count that one as a 'leaner,' like in horseshoes, 'cause we all saw it, That's right, isn't it," consoled John. Al massaged his calf and the pain eased.

"Yeah," added Pete, "that was so close, so close."

It was Bobby who saw another side to the truth. "Geez, Mr. Olsen, I hope that doesn't happen to me. Does fishing get you cramps?" he asked.

Just Keep Going North..

That line brought the grimness to an end. "Yah, Bobby," chuckled Al, "you go fishing with old coots like us, and you'll wind up gettin' cramps all the time. Mostly, we take those cramps home, put 'em in the freezer, and give 'em out for Christmas presents."

The afternoon sun began its powerless descent behind the cloud cover. The grayness in the underbellies of the cloud bank intensified; the waves were now a deep blue-black, with whitish crests. Nearby, gulls were screeching over some tidbit.

Fishing is OK, thought Bobby to himself. I wish I'd get a fish. I wish I could catch one before Gramps. I wish anybody of us would get one. That way, I'd have something to tell David and Tim. They'd never believe I caught a fish. What do I have to do to get one?

It was getting close to mid-afternoon. That coffee had kept John perky, but now the food and drink were reminding him of the due processes of nature. He looked around a bit, and indicated to Al that he was going to make a call back in the woods. That's one of the many euphemisms old-timers use to respond to nature's demands, but that's an issue that might only interest folk anthropologists.

So, John and his roll of toilet paper found a spot a ways back in the woods. There was an old log, devoid of bark and just about as natural a convenience as any sportsman would want. Bears, he thought, that Al Olsen and his stories. Haven't been any bears in these parts for years. Too many people around here for bears.

When John returned to the shore, the first thing he noticed was that the Iowans were gone. They'd left ... finally. The group could fish right where they'd wanted to in the first place. In fact, Al and Pete had already moved down to the point, to the ledge, and were casting eastward into the deeper areas.

"They finally left, I see," remarked John. "Now we can get down to some serious fishing in the time that's left. We can't get skunked this way. It could be the best time of the day, if you can believe those fishing forecasts on TV."

"I guess those people who make up those fishing charts got a direct line to weather, science, and the politicians," added Pete, "but those lines must be busy most of the time. Ya gotta' get a fish to talk and then we'd have some reliable information."

"Where's Bobby?" asked John.

"We thought he was with you," answered Al.

"No. I went over the hill to see a man about a horse. I thought he'd stayed with you guys. I'll go back over to the other side and get him. Watch my line, will ya?"

John walked back from the ledge and climbed over the boulders. Bobby's fishing gear was there, right near the water, and his baseball cap was floating in the water. Where was that kid?

"Bobby? Bobby!" he shouted. No answer. He shouted again, louder. The sound of the wind over-rode his voice. He shouted again. Taking Bobby's fishing pole, he strained to recover Bobby's cap from the lake ... but it was out too far.

Panic hit him. Those Iowans had gone. Where was Bobby? His heart started beating. His mind raced. He ran back to Al, shouting, hollering to be heard against the wind.

"Bobby's gone! He's not over there! We gotta' find him. I gotta find him. His cap was in the water. He coulda' drowned. I couldn't get it out ... it was his cap. We gotta find him fast." John's face was white. His hands shook.

Al and Pete dropped their fishing gear. Together, the three men climbed as fast as they could back to the area they'd fished that morning. There was the blue and white cap still bobbing farther out in the water. Pete ran to edge of the lake trying to see anything that might look like clothing or a body in the water. The blue-blackness of the lake showed nothing; even the boulders were invisible beneath the surface.

"Maybe he just went into the woods to take a pee," suggested Al. "Maybe he'll be back in a few minutes. Kids don't wander off like that without some good reason."

"Yeah, but what about those Iowans? And what's his cap doing in the water? What if they kidnapped him or something like that?" shot back John. "Did you see them leave? Did you notice anything strange about them? Kidnapping kids is ... I can't even say it. I just know something terrible's happened."

The men agreed to split up and begin searching. Al went east along the woodline and shore shouting for Bobby. John went west. Pete covered the area in the middle; they planned to meet at the car in five minutes. If they needed to get help, they'd have to drive about a mile to get to a telephone. Pete would stay back, just in case Bobby reappeared.

Just Keep Going North..

"Bobby, Bobby, where are you?" shouted John as he ran and stumbled along the rocks and boulders that framed the wave-cast shore and woodline.

Three gulls bobbed closer to Bobby's hat, until one hesitantly pecked at it, prompting a squabble over its possession.

"Oh God, oh, Dear Lord, Jesus, don't let this happen," John said to himself. "Take me, if that'd' help. Don't let anything happen to that boy."

"Bobby, Bobby ... Bobby! Answer me! Bobby. Do you hear me?" John's shouts echoed into the ravine near the westerly edge of Stoney Point. Nothing. No signs. Nothing. He'd have to cut through the woods and then get back on the road to the car. He looked back once to see if Bobby might have come back behind him along the shore. Nothing. His breath was coming in gasps.

Tears of frustration and anger started to course down his cheeks. His voice was choked. He could barely shout. What would he tell Marion? What could he possibly say? That he was a stupid old man who couldn't even keep an eye on his grandson. That he was a fool. The police would believe that, all right. How could he face his son and tell him he didn't know what had happened to Bobby. Fishing was a stupid thing to do. He'd never go fishing again. Oh Lord, don't let this happen.

As John broke out of the woods, he could make out the edge of his car, half hidden by brush, about three blocks eastward. Then he saw Al emerge even farther ahead, coming toward him some five blocks away down the road. They both started running toward the car. Where was Pete? Maybe Pete had found the kid. Maybe.

Pete emerged just about where he should have, much closer to the car. He threw out both arms to signal, nothing, didn't see him.

"Any sign of him?" shouted John, but he was too far away to be heard by Pete.

Pete went to the car and opened the door. He spun around and began shouting and waving.

"He's here! He's here!"

And, sure enough, curled up in the backseat was Bobby. The shouting startled him, and he jumped up. "What's the matter?" he asked. "Something wrong? Where's my grandpa?"

Just Keep Going North..

"Listen, boy, your grandpa's goin' to have some things to say to you ... and you'd better listen up. You just about killed that man with worry. Where were you? Why didn't you tell anybody when you left?" cried Pete.

Bobby didn't know why. He just looked down at his boots.

"Oh, Bobby, oh, Bobby," choked out John, "we thought you had drowned. Your cap was floating in the lake."

The tears streamed down his face as he clutched the boy. "Don't you ever do a thing like that again. Never! If you leave, you gotta' tell somebody where you're going and when you'll be back. You can't just walk off. You gotta' tell somebody!" John's body shook with emotion.

Even Al, who was rarely at a loss for words, didn't know what to say. All he could think of was: You better pay attention to your grampa, boy. You gave us a scare like you couldn't believe. If a boy did something like that in the old days, he'd get a thrashing he would remember the rest of his life. He finally said, "You'd better tell your grampa how really sorry you are."

Well, those old gents sure scared the bejeebers out of Bobby. After a few of his own chastened tears, he said he was sorry, but he thought it was all right for him to go to the car. He'd just wanted to get a Hershey bar that he'd squirreled away in the backseat. He musta' fallen asleep. He'd left his cap there to tell them he'd be back. The wind musta' blown it into the lake.

Well, fishing was not the same for the last two hours. Those Iowa fishermen returned; they'd just gone down the road to get some lunch.

Al shared the past hour's events with them and the scare they had. The Iowans kidded Bobby about being lost by himself, which wasn't the same as being lost at all. They seemed not to mind a bit that they'd lost the really good fishing spot. They figured these old guys really had been frightened, and one asked Bobby how he felt about it.

Bobby just shrugged and looked downcast. He guessed this wasn't the time to offer any excuses to anybody.

"How'd you guys like some fish?" asked one of the Iowans. "It seems we can't be sure they'd keep until we get back to 'tall corn

Just Keep Going North..

country.' Maybe you guys could use 'em, seeing's how your luck isn't up to par. That way, you could tell your wives you caught 'em."

"Hells bells," responded John, "how about we invite you folks over to my house and we cook 'em up. It won't take long and that way you get to eat some. I'd guess if we clean 'em up and ask nicely, my wife wouldn't mind too much having to cook. She's a great cook with trout ... broils 'em. Of course, I'm going to ask you guys one thing, and that goes for you, too, Bobby. Nobody says a word about what happened out here, I mean about losing Bobby for a time. That's gotta' stay a secret mostly."

* * *

In bed later that night, John told Marion what had really happened that day. How frightened he was and how mad he got at that kid. Just like his father, he added. And, he said he loved her, and he said he'd tell his favorite daughter-in-law and son what had happened, so Bobby wouldn't be in any trouble. He said she was a wonderful cook and a good wife. And, he hoped she wasn't upset at him for bringing those Iowans and their fish home for dinner. And, he promised Marion that he'd look for some work, maybe some volunteer work over at the church, so he'd get out of her hair. And, he said he loved her again. Marion was loved and she knew it.

That night John dreamt a curious dream. In it, those three Iowans appeared.[*] The older Iowan proposed they all go fishing and would John like to join them; the second Iowan, a bit younger, offered him fishing gear that looked like the newest and the best on the market; he indicated that John could borrow it. The third Iowan held a cooler and minnow bucket.

"Where do you want to go fishing?" asked John They said they knew a great place, kinda' like Lake Superior. Many good-sized trout just waiting to be taken. Why not go with them, they asked. And so he did.

[*] Genesis: 18-2. "And he lifted up his eyes and looked and saw three men standing by him, and when he saw them, he hastened to meet them ...." (In Russian literature, the Old Testament Trinity is symbolized, as to Abraham, by the three strangers made welcome and their gifts.)

Chapter three

The Snow-Birds Are Back

It's been a week that resembles most late March winter weeks in Duluth. Cold and gray. Very little sunshine, mostly gray, with a lot of gray cloud banks that blend into a dull gray landscape. It all adds up to the kind of persistently uniform winter that Duluthians relish and don't seem to get enough of.

On snowbanked street corners motionless Duluthians practice their special rules of social distance and space, waiting for buses that regularly run a few minutes behind schedule. This tardiness seems to be a part of the mission of the Duluth public transit system.

Being tolerably late is, transit-wise, what Duluth bus riders expect. Promptness is what occurs in Milwaukee; San Antonio; even Athens, Georgia; but hardly in Duluth. If Duluth buses were to run on time, riders would be otherwise compensated for fare increases, thereby eliminating a whole range of bus-rider complaints. And, lacking complaints, there'd be nothing whatsoever for bus patrons to grumble about. What you must understand is that Duluthians have their rules for socially acceptable grumbling and bus-stop behavior.

In Duluth, if some stranger — a person you've seen on the same bus stop for fifteen years — should suddenly begin a direct conversation, it had better be about bus service. The only other fit bus-stop topics a Duluthian might dare mention are the weather, potholes in city streets, or maybe the fish-ladder proposed for the Lester River. Anything else would be much too forward for bus-stop patrons, or even for Duluthians as a whole. So, if strangers don't complain about bus service, there's not much else to talk about, anytime, anywhere. Bus talk is designed to keep strangers at arms length, which is proper social distance, rather than sociability.

For bus riders and citizens in general, it's better to nod agreeably but remain silent if a stranger throws a comment your way. That is regarded as a safe, reasonable level of conversation. Most of the time it's better simply to stare at the snowbanks. This tactic discourages further social pleasantries, or emboldened invasions of privacy, which Duluthians learn early to minimize. Bus riding poses

Just Keep Going North..

a continuous test of Duluth upbringing and refinement over the long haul.

Duluthians, especially bus patrons, avoid striking up conversations with strangers, because strangers are essentially unknowable, and are also uncertainties. Duluthians don't begin talking with just anybody about Bergsonian philosophy, gasoline prices, much less televised city council proceedings, for any reason. Those sorts of things just don't happen, at least not within Duluth proper, as any native will grudgingly acknowledge with a shrug.

Behind all of this courtesy is a deeper survival instinct. Duluthians are pretty closemouthed, as bus riders and citizens, because you just don't know with whom you might be talking or how well-placed they could be in Duluth's power structure. In fact, since nobody knows where Duluth's power structure begins or ends, it's just better to keep your mouth shut and your thoughts to yourself. Duluthians figured this all out for themselves some time back; now they zealously practice it since any alternatives are unimaginable. In most situations where the possibility of speaking to a stranger arises, Duluthians would prefer to talk to themselves (and they have a rich inner mental life, filled with fantasies and adventures that take them right to the city limits, but not beyond).

Needless to say, since it goes largely unmentioned, late March is also the time of the year when the bulk of the snow-birds return from Arizona and Florida. These snow-birds typically bring a bagful of complaints back with them from their vacations down South, like how expensive everything was, how the sunshine wasn't quite right, and, of course, how terrible the food was. But, these complaints are reserved mostly for their peers, for kindred snow-birds; it is a simple courtesy not to raise such issues with persons unable to go South to collect such complaints.

You must understand that Duluthians able to venture away during the peak of the winter season could scarcely come back and boast that they weren't in Duluth during the Big Cold and Snow. Naturally, these snow-birds hide their sunburns as best they can by wearing turtleneck sweaters from Phoenix, Dallas, or St. Petersburg, leaving only a facial redness that suggests a degree of embarrassment at having missed the winter season and not having purchased that turtleneck sweater at a local retail store; a redness that could have

Just Keep Going North..

been gotten by overexposure at a local tanning salon. But that's another story.

Upon their return, Duluth snow-birds immediately complain about how they wished they hadn't gone South at all. The misery Duluthians suffer in leaving Duluth, especially in the winter, would in some respects match the sufferings of Job, were it not self-induced. A snow-bird's description of his or her "winter vacation" down South evokes tremendous empathy in most audiences. Most can't even imagine such conditions, leading you to conclude that familiar civilization ends somewhere 148 miles south of the Twin Cities, give or take a few idioms and the northward spread of the drawl.

(Incidentally, Duluthians do not acquire a Southern accent even if they stay close to three weeks in the Sun Belt; the prices they encounter there keep their lips and cheeks pinched too tightly to allow escape of anything more than gasps. Consequently, they don't even hear Southern accents, as their minds are preoccupied with rationing their thoughts and budgeting their vacation dollars.)

Of course, re-entry to Duluth culture and lifestyle for these snow-birds is never easy. To restore their metabolism and psyche, the first thing snow-birds do is head for the Chinese Platter restaurant, down on 4th Avenue West and First Street, to have their faith in real Chinese food restored. It seems Duluthians don't "do Chinese" very often, but when they do, it had better taste like the Chinese Platter's food or it isn't quite right. And, of course, what these snow-birds try to describe as Chinese food down South defies description.

Duluthian's taste buds are programmed quite early in life. If a food is too sweet, or too salty, or has some odd taste or strange texture to it, well, it probably wasn't cooked in Duluth. Mostly, Duluthians like foods with the texture of a stringy beef roast, cooked for five hours at 400 degrees; they like it even better after it's been re-heated the next day, for an hour or so. Naturally, this restricts most adventures in Sun Belt cuisine for snow-irds from Duluth. But adventures outside of Duluth don't have the same cash value as those created locally anyway.

Just Keep Going North..

Chapter four

Sure Are A Lot Of Smart Cats Around Here

Not surprisingly, it's been another sullen-gray March week in Duluth; not too cold though (windchill, minus fifteen degrees) and just a sprinkling of snow to remind everyone that winter will stick around for at least eight more weeks. Not unlike last week, the current week was another remorseless seven days that didn't seem to want to end. It was that kind of slow week that makes Duluthians yearn for those four days of spring in late June. It was the kind of week when thoughts about rotating the tires, re-grouting the bathroom tiles, or carrying those bundled *National Geographic* magazines out to the garage, just pop into people's heads. Strange thoughts start moving in and just take over.

The whole thought process associated with late winter gets a jump start by simply connecting two cables: one goes to the left side of the mind, the negative pole, called "knowing what hasn't been done," while the other cable goes to the positive side, known as "what shoulda' been done." And, sooner than expected, such thought processes unleash the Duluth virtues of guilt, challenge, remorse, and promise of penitent personal development, before it's too late.

For instance, the regular crowd out at the West End VFW Club just sits around trying to be amiable during the happy hour, telling each other about these thoughts, about the things they got to do before winter ends. The accumulated winter tasks have a way of bearing down on the mind, like a twenty-eight inch snow-burden on a hunting shack. And, a lot of people just cave in altogether to these ideas.

It's been the kind of week when some Duluthians get too much practice at dour thinking and reflecting, and spend too much time with thoughts about things they should have done, but didn't quite get around to. Thoughts like, what if they had taken that job down in the Twin Cities and moved — actually picked up and left Duluth, where would they be now? Or thoughts about whether their cabin roof out on Caribou Lake will leak when the snowmelt really begins ... did that tar-paper repair job do the trick or not?

It takes years of practice to deal with these sorts of thoughts because they sneak up on you and anchor near the edge of consciousness, night and day. Getting rid of these thoughts is not easy; they have to be dealt with one at a time, sorted out, and then put way back into one's mental deep-freeze. If ignored, those thoughts will simply wait around until they get some attention. They can jump right out in the middle of a telephone call or even a sales presentation, causing a mental "flutter-by" that can interfere with your entire thought process. Why, these thoughts can be so distracting, it can sometimes take four to five martinis or five or six cups of coffee to sort them all out. Worst of all, they tend to dance around in a person's mind just before bedtime and return around five every morning. For old-time Duluthians, it's worse knowing that these ideas have to be settled before daylight savings time begins, or matters will just start an hour earlier.

Too much thinking along these lines leads many a Duluthian to end-of-winter sulkiness, not just cabin fever. They start thinking about re-painting closets or even starting a new collection of some kind, like old dictionaries, or matchbooks, or something like that. Of course, they snap right back after a weekend down in the Twin Cities; sometimes just thinking about shopping in the Twin Cities cures Duluthians of these end-of-winter thoughts.

Emptying and sorting out the contents of a tackle box is a sure sign of a Duluthian deep in the throes of end-of-winter melancholy. Some people call it brooding, since melancholy isn't treated by physicians in town anymore, those physicians who used to prescribe pep pills year-round for some Duluthians. You'd be surprised how many hours are spent by Duluthians arranging and re-arranging fishing lures and plugs in those green tackle boxes, down in the basement, by themselves, humming a little bit and smiling once in a awhile. This ritual is better than Rolfing for most Duluthians, even better than medicine, and it works most of the time.

One of the neighbors was saying that Carl Hedstrom and his wife — her "go-by" name is Sunny, her real name is Linnea Anne — had been having some trouble getting through the winter lately. Even that trip to Raleigh, North Carolina, to their daughter's place, and being with the grandchildren, didn't help much. Now that Carl is retired, he just mopes around the house and that gets to Sunny; she tries to get him to do things, like walking over to Tara's grocery store for cracked wheat bread and the Inquiring Mind. Mostly, though, he

Just Keep Going North..

just kind of follows her around the house and talks outloud to her about things that cross his mind or sits in the recliner in front of the TV. Sunny finally told him that he was becoming a real nuisance; that she couldn't get her housework done; that he was sure enough becoming just an old man underfoot, like his father was to his mother after he retired. He'd better do something about that and do it in a hurry. You can be sure those sentiments from Sunny hit Carl hard.

After Sunny went after Carl with those words that retired people never want to hear from their spouse, she said she was going over to the Mt. Royale Grocery Store to get a few fresh things, like bread, eggs, a bunch of celery, and a few pork chops, and did he want anything from there?

Naw, he didn't need anything was what she heard from the recliner area in the living room. He just sat there thinking and reviewing matters. He had a lot of dour thoughts on his mind, and he wasn't going to let her call him an old man, a nuisance.... He'd show her who was boss.

Well, while Sunny was gone, Carl took her big sewing bag and dumped out her sewing things all over the floor, spreading the collected tools and materials of her hobby all around the dining room and carpeted hallway. He even unrolled several balls of yarn and then just waited for her to get back. He just sat there, grim-faced and tense. Imagine, Sunny telling him he was underfoot. He'd show her a thing or two.

You can just guess how shocked Sunny was when she walked into her dining room and saw her sewing things helter-skelter — her favorite pinking shears out of their case, her tomato-shaped pincushions smiling at her, her buttons and yarn everywhere, and her big spools of thread all over the place. She was as crazed as Michelangelo might have been if someone had come in and splashed white paint all over the ceiling of the Sistine Chapel and then added strobe lights. Her barely started wall-hanging sampler, with the words: "Need a Hand: Look at the End of Your Arms," was crumpled, its many, colored yarns, ravaged. She slammed that bag of groceries down on the kitchen counter so hard that even the glasses in the dishwasher felt her anger. The knives in their cutlery holders almost turned into spoons to avoid what they knew was coming.

"I can't even leave you alone for an hour to go to the store," she yelled at Carl."I come back and find this ... this mess all over the downstairs." Sunny was in no mood to hear any explanations.

"It musta' been the cat. Yep, it coulda' been the cat got into those things while I was takin' a nap," said Carl from his recliner. And that was all that passed between those persons married for more than forty years. Not too much was said about that episode at dinner, although you can bet things were a bit quieter than usual, and the pork chops were a bit scorched, at least those served Carl. Not as many opinions were expressed at that dinner, not about the Duluth economy, not about their trip down to North Carolina; even their sons-in-law caught much less flak that night. It was just the tail-end of winter in Duluth getting to people. Imagine, after all those years.

It seems the next day the Hedstrom's cat got into Carl's green fishing tackle box and made quite a mess of it. It appears that cat spread those lures and leaders, plugs and flies, and fishing tackle helter-skelter around the basement floor, even into the carpeted three-quarter bath. Pale blue nylon six pound fishing line was crisscrossed everywhere, except around the Singer sewing machine area. I heard that Carl's favorite walleye plugs, his expensive but proven Rapalla's, got a few nicks in 'em, and that it took him about six hours just to re-arrange the whole thing, all four tiers of the tackle box storage sections for plugs and lures, back to the way he liked them. He never did get all that fishing line untangled.

"It's funny how that cat could unlock the cabinet, lift that thirty-five pound tackle box down to the floor, and then pry open the safety on my tackle box," remarked Carl as he sat down with his wife for a 10:00 a.m. cup of coffee. It was not a bit strange to Sunny, not at all; why she'd heard about a cat on the next block, over there to the west, that had been trained to take out the garbage — that cat over at Anderson's, the Anderson who works for the Buick dealership in town; and she'd even heard of a cat out in Lakeside that had been taught to bring in the mail. It seems Sunny had an unspoken treasury of cat stories, about how smart cats really are, as compared with other critters.

And, that's how some Duluthians play the game of winter-ending. It's a fun game, but nobody keeps score. So, just remember, there sure are a lot of smart cats in Duluth and you'd better keep your tackle box away from them, or Lord knows what will happen next.

Just Keep Going North..

Chapter 5

Guess Who I Am & What I Do?

Most news stories originating in Duluth don't make much sense unless tracked right down to their roots, plus some thirty feet deeper, to get to bedrock, which is close to where this story begins.

It seems that some six months back the City Personnel, Training, & Job-Development department head contracted with two consultants. (It should be obvious why consultants come to Duluth in pairs: one is related to some official or has over-bubbling political influence, while the other writes the invoice for services on a lap-top computer to expedite payment.) It seems these out-state consultants had found a vein of ore in Duluth so to speak, in the inexperience and desire of the city and its human resource director to keep Duluth abreast of new management practices, all of which gives new and profound meaning to the term extraction economics, at least to these consultants.

Of course, these consultants came well recommended, all the way from Pittsburgh via Minneapolis, through Wausau to Duluth, having worked their way through the Iron Range and its Rehabilitation Council.

Given their expense account latitude, these consultants absolutely dazzled the department director and his task force with their cogent vocabulary, their hi-tech sense of applications and concepts, not to mention their key contacts in industry and public sector — the latter being repeatedly mentioned over drinks down at the Holidaze Inn.

Rarely before had the Director heard such terms, such as "just-in-time/just-in case," explained so lucidly. Other concepts flowed forth from the lips of these consultants, as if they were imitating a state senator, or even Minnesota's governor. Through the sincerity of their efforts and sheer brilliance, the city management training needs were exposed and its coffers pried open.

The entire collection of ideas and practices was available for a mere $78,500, which included 800 copies of a compelling literary effort in human relations, the intellectual product of several brains in human resource management, entitled "Zipff: How to Do it

Just Keep Going North..

Managerially in Less than 15 Minutes, with Time to Spare for Improving Productivity, Quality & Profits Over-Nite in Service & Product Systems."

This was certainly what the Director needed; he was ready to begin reading "See Spot run. See Jane run," if that was what it took to enhance human resource management enterprises in Duluth, and apparently it took just that. "Needs assessment and new ideas should not be gauged by the Flesch test," is what he suggested to his Human Resources Task Force.

But, ideas like these pose deep questions. The question was which idea to start with and then how to make it work in Duluth. This called for some broad imagination, because other cities might be attempting these same ideas before Duluth. Image, capacity, learning and delivery factors, potentialities and power were at stake.

Needless to say, having bought that package of "great ideas in management," the city's human resource director was not going to let them go to waste. But, applying those ideas depends upon approval, approval from the right people in city hall, a process more complicated than canonization, and with no fewer miracles required. Approval meant presenting those ideas in their most glittering form to the rank and file worker's councils, the unions, the grievance committees, the city administration, and even to the City Council. It was no snap, but in almost no time that cafeteria of management ideas was ready to be served up.

Of all the ideas, the union membership felt that "just-in-time" or JIT, as they called it, was the classiest; it sounded good and had a certain crispness, which are not strange criteria for gauging ideas, at least not in Duluth. If you still don't have a sense of how things really work in Duluth city services, you'd better be prepared for some strange twists and curves ahead.

In the hands of those eager Duluth city employees, JIT came to mean getting the work done "just in time." In the licensing bureau, JIT meant that the clerk sat a few seconds, or even a few minutes longer, until a look of agonized impatience settled grimly on the face of the citizen-customer. In the City Assessor's Office, it meant mailing the homestead notices just two days before they were due back in January. And, in the Purchasing Department, it meant delaying supply re-orders right down to the stock-out point, almost achieving

Just Keep Going North..

a zero-based inventory, which isn't all bad unless a person really needs a blank piece of paper.

Naturally, all of the departments cooperated with the JIT program, since it was so close to how they operated normally; it was like doing what they were supposed to do in the first place, but now it had a name. And, in Duluth, when something gets named, it not only signals a problem, but also the solution. It's fair to say that JIT swept city hall like a well-worn broom. Payroll authorizations were delayed right down to the last minute, earning close to $ 1,105.83 in heretofore lost daily interest.

Of course, the Fire Department handled the program a bit differently. Those Fire Fighting units put wholehearted emphasis on the "just-in-case-of-fire" part of JIT. As everybody now knows, just-in-case meant the Fire Department created regular routes across the city for fire detection and response. Those fire rigs would go slowly through the neighborhoods on their routes, sirens blaring, looking for fires. Cellular phones sped up communications between 911 and the fire truck. But if there was going to be a fire, it had better be along a route scheduled for that day, and it had better be during normal business hours, since the routing schedule was balanced nicely against the fire-hall cooking schedules and cribbage contests.

Some persons phoning in fire alarms were asked if they could keep the fire under control for a bit, since their burning house wasn't on the regular just-in-case-of-fire route until later in the afternoon. All told, I guess stacking up those fire calls made a lot of sense, as opposed to suiting up and then dashing out here and there to put out fires. It just made more sense to batch them up and handle them all at one time, just-in-time and just-in-case, which Duluthians seemed to accept as part of cost-reduction in services and focused productivity planning.

Likewise, snow removal occurred right at the peak of snow accumulation; no need to do it earlier when you can do it just-in-time. The savings in service dollars were fantastic. The City Council was astounded at the savings and efficiency. Since those city officials knew there was no way to inventory services, the next best thing was to adopt a flexible delay in delivery, and that's why JIT succeeded so well. It was a principle, when carefully customized to services, that was clearly made for Duluth.

Just Keep Going North..

The stream of management ideas seemed inexhaustible. When it came to KANBAN, the second runner-up in that flood of new management ideas, the imagination of those city employees was positively unbounded. Expensive KANBAN carts were placed outside each department's quarters; the carts had been purchased from the Toyota-Takahishi Company Auto Plant in Janesville, Wisconsin, and custom painted to match the art deco in city hall. After all, if one is going to practice KANBAN, the idea is to do it right the first time.

KANBAN was a real hit; it worked as follows. Each employee wrote in his or her coffee-break order anytime before 9:30 a.m. and again before 2:30 p.m. The lists and KANBAN carts were moved from department to department, after which they were hustled over to the cafeteria. Each cart was filled with French pastries, Swedish and Danish smorgasbord items, German cakes, plus real Columbian and Vienna-style coffee, and then whisked back to the waiting employees. Morale soared, even if productivity suffered a bit, since employees competed to see who could come up with the most exotic menus for future weeks. Things were taking a direction unheralded in the design of employee benefits, anywhere, anytime, not to criticize Duluth's deserving city employees for recognizing a need and taking affirmative action. After-hours aerobics fit in quite well, too, since a few employees began developing slight paunches, what with all those calorie-laden coffee breaks.

But, then, as things must, the really sticky management idea surfaced. It had to do with work analysis and job design, which is after all what most management ideas are all about anyway. This concept got right down to the people level and what work would really mean for each city employee. Thinking this idea through took a lot of meetings and a lot of proper group dynamics done in just the right way.

For starters, Elaine Mulvahill, over in City Tax Collections, wanted to design her job around the identity of Marilyn Monroe. She was tired of being just "plain old Elaine." She thought her job called for enticing money out of reluctant taxpayers. She thought people might be more willing to pay their taxes promptly if they got a little "charming invitation," along with the whole works. Well, that didn't seem too unreasonable, not at all. It even gave those other city employees in the focused work analysis team something to think about that night. True, some of them had a bit of difficulty squeezing Elaine into their mental image of Marilyn Monroe. But, upon closer

Just Keep Going North..

thought, maybe that wasn't what they were supposed to do. Maybe they were supposed to let their personal identity fill up and expand job design, given their talents, experience, and whatever else they had to work with.

So, at the next focused work analysis team meeting, Lance Rutherford, who works down in Central Accounting Records in the basement of city hall, a shy fellow, said he wanted to be something like Tom Cruise, Vanilla Ice, and John Houston, or close to that. It's hard to say because Lance speaks so softly, and the neighbors got all this insider information secondhand. Lance felt that his job needed more glamour and appeal. He even wrote out a job script, including the deep-voiced telephone replies he would use. A few eyebrows were raised, but overall no one objected. If this was what job design and enrichment was all about, well, perhaps it was a bit too early to be critical. After all, Duluth streets weren't bricked in a day and Rome wasn't built in a year, as they say in Duluth. Maybe those people who keep poking fun at Duluth wouldn't be so critical, at least not when they saw how much improvement could result from these scientifically and humanistically designed jobs.

However, when Sandra ("Sandy") Engstrom said her job identity should be like the Lester River, because being a clerical support person in the City Legal Department was a swift-moving experience — where you had to learn to move with the flow, take deep plunges, and hold your breath, well, at that point a few persons started looking down at their shoes and squirming. But no one laughed out loud. Everyone just sat there stone-faced and tight-lipped. The consultant praised Sandy for being so open with the group, adding that surely some buoyancy and riparian factors could be designed into her job to give it more current meaning and depth.

Ernie Gustafson couldn't let a moment like this go by, so he signaled to his buddy, Pete Ellerby, that this might be a good time to take a break. Outside the meeting room, on their way to the john, Ernie let rip. "That Sandy, oh boy, you can be sure she'd wanta' be Lester River — high in the spring, icy-dicey to everybody year-round, and no fishin' beyond a quarter mile upstream."

Needless to say, these kinds of reactions to work analysis and group processing were always few and far between, and always rejected, so you could safely conclude that sexism was completely and assuredly on its deathbed somewhere in Duluth.

Just Keep Going North..

The psychodynamics of job re-design proceeded forward since there was no other direction it could go. And, all of this effort had to result in something, because once a commitment is made in Duluth, it is obvious that there must be something to show for it. Excuses, even anticipating failure, don't work in Duluth as they do elsewhere to prompt a halt to matters. Things here must go on to their bitter end, like winter.

Last Wednesday, the results were about to be revealed. Something was going to happen that had never happened before, at least not in Duluth. As city employees arrived at work, each was given a three-and-a-half-inch oval button to wear (pretty much required wearing). Across the upper part of the button in a splash of blue-lettering were the words:

I'M A DULUTH CITY

EMPLOYEE!

And in a neatly curved arc below, in very a modern Swiss font, was the question:

GUESS WHO I AM & WHAT I DO?

Of course, some of the Public Works folks wore those button under their jackets; if they stopped for a shorty out at the Western Bar, they didn't want any wisecracks from other patrons. City Planning Department personnel wore their buttons clipped to their U.S.A. hats. It seems the folks over in the City Legal Department had trouble with the safety clasps on the back of their buttons, even going so far as to suggest the buttons were cheaply made. A few of those lawyers wound up using Scotch Magic mending tape to hold those buttons in place, which is what could happen when too much is asked of lawyers by way of hand-eye coordination skills.

Well, Elaine Mulvahill sauntered up to her counter in Tax Collections last Wednesday at about 8:15 in the morning, having rehearsed her script for several hours on Tuesday night with Rita-Jane Grochowski. They wanted to get it down and get it right. Actually, with only modest bending of the imagination, at forty-nine, Elaine did a fair imitation of Marilyn Monroe, although some of the effect would naturally be lost to the untrained eye. Age seemed to have created more uphill contouring with Elaine than with most of her peers. Mother nature seemed determined to keep her firmly positioned in a shapely, but definitely Rubenesque, genre. For her age she was a doll and she knew it. Standing there at the counter was

Just Keep Going North..

Mr. Kenneth Bjorklund, seventy-six years old, semi-retired, but still active in real estate sales. He wanted to pay his tax on a used car he'd purchased.

"Guess who I am and what I do?" smarmed Elaine, giving her most sultry imitation of Monroe, including the pursed lips and light fingertip touch to her bouffant wig. After all, if the public was going to benefit from job enrichment, it had better get used to the new image and approach sometime. The Duluth public had to realize that city employees were people, too, with needs for challenges, and a zest for power, recognition, and new experiences.

"For heaven's sakes, you're Elaine Mulvahill, and you've worked here, I'd guess, for about twenty-two years. Your parents live over on Chester Park Drive and...."

But before old Mr. Bjorklund could say more (he already said what was a mouthful of words for him anyway, since for forty-five years he'd mostly sold houses with the fewest words possible), Elaine burst out with: "Nope, not anymore! This is the *real* me. I'm a new person. I'm a sultry, compliant civil servant, hoping to make your tax payments more fun, even easier, by *enticing* that money out of you, and giving some *extra service* in return, if you get my drift? It's all part of image-building for the Tax Department, and job enlargement for me."

The thoughts that crossed that seventy-six-year-old man's mind! The affront was unimaginable. You can believe Bjorklund's face turned red; he was embarrassed for himself and for this young lady he'd known since birth. His heart started pumping, his eyes and dentures both clamped down at the same time, and his breathing hurt.

He was barely able to stammer out, "Why, Elaine Mulvahill, I never thought you, of all persons, would turn out to be a ...." He didn't know what to say next. But neither did he get a chance to finish that sentence. Elaine just turned away from the trembling figure of old Mr. Bjorklund, and ambled along the counter to the next person.

Bjorklund just stood there, checkbook and tax notice in hand, shaking. He felt Elaine's father, Joe Mulvahill, would die a hundred deaths if he knew what his daughter was doing, right there at the Tax Collections counter. But he wasn't going to be the one to tell him. He'd just pretend it didn't happen. He'd come back tomorrow, after he'd had a chance to discuss the matter with his wife. It would probably take him a bit longer to drive back up Chester Park Drive. Once home, he'd get a cup of coffee before he told his wife, Elsie, what he'd experienced. She'd probably say it was just an old man's imagination. But it wasn't. It was true, and it was more than he could handle.

"Next! Next person! Guess who I am and what I do?" demanded Elaine, exuding Monroe-like charm and grace to the next customer. She'd been told that solid job enlargement and enrichment took perseverance, and she wasn't going to let this one encounter block her efforts to ascend the ladder in Tax Collections. At least not somebody like old Mr. Bjorklund. She knew the telephone lines would behumming soon enough within the geriatric network. But that's the price one has to pay to succeed in the public sector these days, Elaine thought to herself.

Well, the neighbors said similar things were going on all over Duluth last Wednesday. Old friendships were broken in a matter of minutes, and residents tried to figure out who and what this new breed of civil servants was all about and why. For some Duluthians, it appeared the implausible had collided with the improbable and events simply had to take their usual downhill course. One meter reader tried out his new job-identity approach on Mrs. Kathyrin Schmidt, out there on Crescent View Drive. She's fifty-two, a recent widow, but a pretty classy lady. She hit that meter reader over the head with the end of her Sears vacuum attachment and let loose a string of words, the likes of which that meter reader thought people on Crescent View Drive shouldn't even know.

By 2:00 p.m., the mayor's office had received just enough complaints, about 4:38, the Mayor's popularity and problem-solving meter reached the "must take action or else" level and was heading for the red zone, labeled "CRISIS IN DULUTH," where just plain muddling through wouldn't work. The Mayor decided action was the better part of managing chaos, so take action he did. He called the director of City Personnel, Training, and Job-Development, and told him he'd better get down to his office right away, yes, today, and before 3:30 this afternoon, if not sooner.

The Mayor listened to what the Director had to say, since that didn't cost anything. He listened just long enough to hear "Guess Who I Am and What I Do?", before he started laughing. And he

Just Keep Going North..

laughed and laughed; tears began leaking from the corners of his eyes and he could scarcely get the following words out.

"You're Elmer Peterson, you're my sister-in-law's cousin, and you've just been officially suspended ... fired!"

"Ooh, yea?!" tossed back Elmer. "Just remember this, *your honor* ... guess who the next mayor's goin' to be in this town and who's goin' to make it happen! You're the guy that set me up for this job and I got lotsa' things that people in this town might wanna' hear!"

Well, it seems city officials are still trying to sort out that experiment of tried and untried tricks from the bagful of management concepts those consultants managed to sell the director. Right now, about forty-five city employees have voluntarily submitted themselves for counseling and occupational therapy. It appears some of them were psychologically damaged during the job enrichment and implementation phase, which is going to cost the city health benefits program a few bucks.

But things did turn out well for some people. Elaine Mulvahill discovered that her talents were far more welcome over in Superior, with the Douglas County Tax Payments Department. Those "flat-landers" sure know a good thing when they see it. She now heads the department and is making quite a hit with her tax-enticing routine.

As for those 868 "Guess Who I Am & What I Do" buttons, well, those were all collected and donated to the Girl Scouts. With some masking tape to cover the splashy blue lettering on the top, the buttons boost cookie sales. It seems those buttons are ice-breakers, especially for the shyer girls. Cookie sales are well above last year's, and so is the cheer and good humor these Girl Scouts bring to their door-to-door sales.

Chapter six

If Summer Arrives This Year, You'll Be First To Know

It's getting close to that time of year in Duluth that's euphemistically called summer. Of course, by any accepted standards it's called summer most every place else, but then it's also more likely *to be* summer elsewhere. In Duluth, those 18.4 days of summer, starting perhaps around June 28 and extending through most of July, have to be crammed full of everything one would normally do over some sixty to ninety days, except in the polar regions. Summer is not the apogee of Duluth's seasons; every Duluthian knows mid-winter, with its minus seventy windchill, is the high point. Winter is a season and a half, while summer is only the hinge between spring and fall.

Nonetheless, this brief period in Duluth is called summer because it dramatizes the persistent hopes of the few rising above the unfulfilled aspirations of the many. The hope is that summer will arrive with some uncommon weather and that it might linger around at least until August 5. The alternative is an extended spring, with rain, fog, early frost, and, probably, an early autumn.

Duluthians and their summer aspirations deserve more than casual comment. After all, the ability to shift from impudent disdain for winter into a wary uncertainty of summer alone qualifies Duluth for a Star City Survivor Plaque, but probably not a Baldrige Quality Award based on customer satisfaction or quality control. Robust survival strategies are born and tested in Duluth, but, unfortunately, no one appears to keep score. Maybe Duluth, like the Serengeti Plain, is a living laboratory planned long ago for the study of climactic effects on humans, a piece of the planet fated to be the de-stabilizing factor in the Gaea model.

It could be. Stranger things have been said about Duluth. The downtown could surely represent economic melt-down, a localized version of architectural/aesthetic fallout. Some Duluth solons certainly do resemble blast victims of the excessive intellectual demands and overexposure to political realities in down-state legislative sessions.

Just Keep Going North..

Some Duluthians escape their regular earth-bound homes around Memorial Day (which is also designated as Ice-Out Day on the Big Lake). About that time, some Duluthians begin to haul out their families, food-packs, twelve-packs, motors, boats, and fishing tackle and head for the cabin. Driven either by instincts or hormones that prompt a return to using even more primitive survival techniques than those required in town, Duluthians head for the cabin, determined to have some fun this summer in the worst way.

For those able to afford a retreat from Duluth, cabin life has many justifications. To Duluthians, a cabin is rustic proof of the continuity of generations. It is proof that a site and a family can be under continuous improvement and upgrading — from the original one-room, pine log structure, complete with kerosene lamps, outhouse, and outdoor pump built by yesteryear's generation, to the present indoor facilities, barbecue and patio, sixty-foot dock, pontoon boat, and solar heating. A cabin is proof that twenty to twenty-four people can be accommodated as easily as four to six people, providing the regular rules of life in Duluth are suspended momentarily.

The cabin is a rustic retreat rarely more than thirty-five minutes from Duluth. And, imagine! All of this effort, this "continuously under-improvement activity" on a half-acre in the northwoods, is what appeals to Duluthians as an escape from the pressures of life in Duluth.

Some Duluthians take advantage of a relative's cabin, usually an in-law's place, with the understanding that with the invitation comes several obvious obligations, such as to join the gang in cleaning out the old septic system, re-roofing some part of the structure, building an addition to the always too small kitchen, or adding another story or two. Summer is filled with doing things at the cabin that people would never do at home in Duluth, if they knew other people were watching. Duluthians most resemble other people when they are out of town or at the cabin.

It should be no surprise, then, to hear a married daughter confront her mother with: "Geez, Mom, I never thought you and Dad did *those things* ... you sure don't do that back home in Duluth, at least not that we kids ever learned about!"

There are several reasons why Duluthians — living in the midst of parks, pines, and birch, facing the largest freshwater lake in

Just Keep Going North..

the world — feel the soul-deep need to escape to a mosquito and deerfly-ridden, muck-bottomed, leech-infested lake, to a place the DNR promises annually to re-stock with northerns and walleye. (Few, if any, living persons have ever seen DNR personnel at these inland lakes over the past forty-five years, but rumors persist that adjacent lakes are re-stocked regularly.) Summer-inspired hopes die slowly in the North Country. Duluthians don't head for those inland lakes just to catch some of those DNR people offguard, in the act of really managing fish, which would be a little like snaring the Easter Rabbit or netting Santa Claus.

The real reason Duluthians leave town during the summer, imaginary or real, is the need to escape from what's going to happen in Duluth, what's supposed to happen, and how it could affect them.

Some Duluth professional types leave town because business comes to a near stand-still anyway, since everybody else is leaving town. Others, of course, don't like to deal with the intense tourist pressure and their businesses don't depend on tourists. Duluthians really can't handle tourists, especially the fisher folk from Iowa, Nebraska, Michigan, or Illinois. Why, the way those tourists spend their money for gaudy fishing tackle and lures, for fluorescent-painted doodads and bobbers, and the fishing outfits they wear, well, it's all Duluthians can do to keep a straight face.

"Hey, does this Boopsy-Whopper really catch fish?" asked the Nebraskan, the one sporting a fish net on his belt and wearing the hat decorated with fake Joe Grunseth trout flies.

"Oh, you bet," answered the clerk, "why I heard tell they've been really hittin' on those things. You oughta' get two or three, and have you got a Redy-Angler's Swizzle-Stick-Popper for rock bass and perch? They're the best. We musta' iced twelve cases of rock bass last week, and shipped it down south. Where you from, mister?"

"Nebraska, right outside Lincoln. Ever heard of Nebraska, boy? Big wheat country, lotsa' wheat, but we don't have the fishin' country like you got up here."

Ya, I know where Nuu-graska is," said the twenty-year-old clerk at the Greatest Little Tackle & Minnow Shop, adding that the customer probably didn't have mosquitoes down there as big as those grown up near Rice Lake.

"You should really get some mosquito netting, and some of this bug repellent. And, I suppose you know how dangerous those

Just Keep Going North..

armyworms are. You oughta' get a complete first-aid kit. One of the other people working here had to rush a friend right down to St. Luke's Hospital, 'cause he got right in the midst of those *armyworms* ... kinda' like what happened overseas with the recent war, you know, the military, armyworms, lotsa' pain."

Well, about $175.41 later, that Nebraskan was sure ready to catch fish. And that clerk was ready to catch another tourist.

Overall, the California tourists are the worst, what with all their "spendy" spending money, laid-back talk, and self-willed contentment. Duluthians have a hard time relating to those types. And when those tourists start taking pictures of Duluthians, asking them to pose by those old-fashioned buildings downtown, and asking them to smile and look happy, well, that really gets to Duluthians. They want to get right out of town, to a woodsy place, where they can be their dour, minimal selves. They don't want to look happy for tourists; they don't appreciate tourists coming into town and making remarks about how quaint things are, what an "unusual paving job" was done just with those curious bricks for roadway material, and how much planning and work must go into keeping the downtown area in such a carefully thought-out deteriorated condition. "Active history," is what one tourist called it, as she stumbled along the bricked sidewalk.

Duluthians don't take too kindly to such comments about their city. After all, residents are regularly reminded by city officials that Duluth is a pretty good place to live. Who do tourists think they are to doubt such insider information? Some judgments about Duluth are better left suspended, at least until after one dies, when a person can evaluate and form a reasonable opinion. Every Duluthian understands this to be the preferred civic philosophy and approach.

For the rest of the Duluthians on whom summer descends, aspirations are mostly funneled into four nearly compulsory outlets: "clumping," "splitting," the minor sports, and the major social class events. Anything else that goes on in Duluth, well, you'll have to figure out for yourself what it could be and what it means.

Clumpers spend their time inspecting, re-seeding, and watering vast clumps of winter-killed grass on the downhill side of yards where grass was never meant to grow. They spend a good portion of their summer worrying about clumps of lilacs, iris, peonies, pole beans, and re-planted arborvitae, wondering if they will survive another winter like the past one.

Clumpers usually wear distinctive costumes to signal their outdoor activities and purpose, because sometimes a passerby might confuse them with very fancy yard sculptures, even scarecrows. Clumpers don't move very fast, and when leaning on a rake or bent over a bed of iris, they actually resemble the new forms of lawn ornamentation. Clearly, their garb suggests a down-to-earth attitude toward the greening of America, toward their grass, shrubs, and gardens. This is summer work and should never be equated with some recreational activity. Male clumpers tend to go for khaki or green shirts and pants, a John Deere cap, and a sweat-filled brakeman's handkerchief hanging out the backpocket. Female clumper folk go more for oversized gray shirts, jeans, wide-brimmed straw hats, and boots or overshoes.

Clumpers spend a great deal of time noisily moving their collection of gardening tools and equipment from the garage to the yard, which is what clumping around is all about. They spend even more time in the patient selection of the right tool for the right job. Clumpers talk to themselves a great deal, but this is simply their way of playing out their script, a way of announcing to anyone within hearing distance what they're going to do next, why, and how. This gives due notice to family members that they should be out there helping and doing their bit to improve the environment.

Clumpers really know how to manipulate guilt, status demands, and eco-values to make non-participating family members miserable. The idea is to make the improbable possible so that it stands out as a positive Northland yard or garden achievement. Able clumpers can set family relations back to the Dark Ages by muttering and grumbling about the lack of support for all their efforts. If unsuccessful in gaining family backing, clumpers later relate minute by minute, task by task, what they did, what their hopes are, and what's going to happen next, as a means of conning others into their endless yard and garden activities. For clumpers, planning the next move, discussing failures and yard problems with neighbors, and exchanging folklore about winterkill is about as exciting as things get. In fact, a whole Duluth summer can go by with clumpers mostly just talking about aphids, rose wilt, tomato grub worms, or voles. It seems that's how clumpers get things done. Overall, clumpers really don't

Just Keep Going North..

want solutions, not when problems are the main source of their fulfillment and summer joy.

Splitters, on the other hand, take their stance more literally. They can't wait to get out to their cabin or woodlot, permit in hand, to start knocking down a few trees, hauling off the occasional windfall, and stashing away a wood supply for next winter. The summer is spent splitting up last year's seasoned wood.

Real splitters are known by the woodpiles they keep. Around the Head-O-The-Lakes, only three patterns count for anything: the "quasi-Finnish," clearly identified by its radiating cones of split logs — Red Finns cut logs to thirty-seven centimeters, while White Finns pretty much stick to sixteen inches; the "semi-Swedish," built upon a layered, crisscross or herringbone pattern; and the "pseudo-Norwegian," distinctive in terms of its sheer volume of odd-sized kindling and split firewood, plus its creative, helter-skelter arrangement. Most Duluthians understand the phrase, "let the chips fall where they may," to refer to the design scheme of the pseudo-Norwegian woodpile. The semi-Swedish firewood stack is evidently the most serviceable since it allows the wood to breathe, which mentally takes a bit of getting used to. A really dedicated splitter can spend maybe six hours arranging a semi-Swedish woodpile, and you can be sure the neighbors will notice it. Such a woodpile might even bring tourists out to photograph this lost art, much to the splitter's embarrassment.

* * *

In late spring, Duluthians who stick around turn to major and minor events. There's the bar and restaurant-sponsored ball clubs, golf leagues, public and private tennis clubs. An elderly lady, known only as "Grandma," sponsors a marathon, a race that requires runners to dash toward Duluth, when any sane person would have enough sense to run the other way.

What most outsiders don't know about Duluth is its ability to create summer events that have purely local significance, plus a dash of spiritual challenge, with the utmost aim of attracting tourists.

For example, "calming the waters" is a sport peculiar to Duluth. Confined mostly to certain enterprising athletes as a sort of faith-testing experience, and peaking in popularity sometime between 1929 and 1983, the sport has never attracted any real ticket sales.

Calming the waters contenders dress as each sees fit to represent a figure from the New Testament. The attire may frequently be extended to carrying a copy of Scripture or whatever other sacramental the participant wishes to have along on board. The event is held sixty feet from shore, down on Park Point, on the lakeside, when a northeast wind creates waves at least eight feet high. Scheduling the events and practice is uncertain at best.

Equipped with a paddle and a home-made replica of a Galilean fishing boat, each participant sculls to the starting marker. Once signaled by the referee, the athletes stand up in their boats and try to remain standing as long as possible, nearly motionless, against the surging waves. The object is to be calm, prayerfully upright, and to look eastward over the waters; excessive use of the arms or legs, or other body movement for balance, even loud talking, disqualifies a person.

This sport perfectly embodies Duluth values. The contests clearly helped many young persons to become upright citizens of Duluth, closemouthed in the face of adversity, and able to enjoy cold showers in later life.

Over the years, the event had a dedicated following, at least until a number of aspiring politicians and surfers got into the act. The politicians immediately wanted to change the rules, such that verbal attack on the morals and ethics of competitors could be used to distract opponents and cause their downfall. The surfers wanted to add canoes and kayaks, which would clearly dilute the spiritual symbolism of the game.

Few tourists get to see this event anymore. If they do, they may confuse it with the Marine Reserves practicing a Mideastern beach landing, or Treasury agents dressed as Shriners attempting to prevent smuggling of Canadian whisky into the States. Then, too, some Duluthians thought it best to drop out of the sport since some of those plastic boat replacements lacked authenticity and sort of spoiled the interplay of athlete and environment, along with the basic hydrodynamics of the craft.

The more dignified North Country sport is, of course, stone-skipping and the informal stone-skipping contests. Stone-skipping, or "pluffing," originated in Ireland, where it became a means of

Just Keep Going North..

expressing civil disobedience and unrest when folk dancing, procreation, and "wearin' o' the Green" were banned. Much earlier, stone-skipping was a Celtic custom, a sexual invitation initiated by a shy, usually unmarried woman, whose gesture required the man to skip his stones across the water more times than she had. Pluffing, and a lot of it, signaled his acceptance of her invitation. Celtic legends relate that women were notoriously poor stone-skippers, but they tried their best, which may partially explain Celtic/Irish survival if such legends have any truth to them.

By 908 A.D., the custom of stone-skipping had spread northward from Ireland to Scandinavia, carried on the waves of returning Vikings, where the idea skipped along quite nicely. Those Irish lassies must have taught the Vikings a trick or two, after all. Among the Scandinavians, however, stone-skipping became a non-verbal means for reducing spousal conflict; that spouse whose stone skipped the most times won the unvoiced argument. It was an ideal solution for those inner-directed, conflict-avoidant Scandinavians as their Viking bloodlines wore thin. So, the custom reached the North Country, and stone-skipping was taught by mothers to daughters, by fathers to sons, even though the original intent was somewhat lost during migration.

Results of stone-skipping contests can give unprecedented social status to the victor. Pluffing begins when someone in the household suggests that maybe they should take a trip up the North Shore. Implied is the notion that it's time to search for some really good skipping stones. The good stones are round and thin; elliptical stones are best, with a slight upward contour toward the center. Every Duluthian knows what a good skipping stone looks like, but they pretty much keep this information to themselves.

The contest rules can get a little complicated. Older men rarely play against each other, since the loser's skipping count is interpreted against a sexual vigor standard, e.g., "What's the matter ... you've got no 'pluff' left in ya anymore?" or "Ya, well, that just shows how your pluff stands." Older men prefer pluffing to end in a stalemate to preserve the remnants of a psychosexual identity in retirement and to provide the basis for a rematch. Women rarely suggest a contest with each other. It's OK for a child to challenge a parent, but the child always skips first. Men initiate the contest and non-verbally invite their mate or a person they wish to challenge. A sister-in-law can compete against her brother-in-law, providing the contest ends in a tie; if either party wins, it means trouble. Sisters-in-law can fill in for each other to uphold female status, but brothers-in-law cannot substitute for each other, since that would reduce the status of the male challenge. Everybody gets five turns, and only the highest number of pluffs count.

On Sunday last week, Helga ("Bunny") Johannson beat her husband at skipping stones, right out there at French River, just twenty yards east of the mouth of the river where the shoreline is filled with pebbles and pretty good skipping stones. It wasn't a real contest: they didn't have any unsettled problems, but now they did. Bunny wasn't supposed to win, she wasn't even supposed to get into *that* family pluffing contest, not at all. But she did. And, with those nine visiting relatives from Racine, Wisconsin, and her brother egging her on, she just went ahead and did it anyway.

Conrad Johannson wasn't happy about losing face in front of his in-laws. He'd given Bunny a signal that she was supposed to "leave off" after her third stone skipped twelve times. Conrad found a flat, round stone that fit just perfectly in his hand. The relatives, including Bunny's brother, sensed a real contest emerging. The kids were finding stones and saying, "Here Aunt Bunny, try this one," or "Here, Uncle Conrad, use this one ... it's perfect."

Of course, some of the in-laws were half-heartedly trying out their skills, but not throwing down any real challenges. Bunny's sister skipped a fourteen, which is pretty good. Conrad brought his arm back, crouched, and spun an underarm pluff that bounced off a wave and then began a series of rapid skips; the stone sped forward, cresting once, twice, ... until it petered out with what the official counter said was sixteen skips.

Helga's brother next got the skip count up to eighteen. Now, it was Bunny's turn again. She picked up a thin clamshell-shaped piece of waterworn basalt, settled it in her hand, brought back her arm, and threw. That stone skipped twenty-two times. As she later told her cousin, "Ya, well, you hafta' understand, Conrad and I come out here a lotta' times just to watch the lake and skip stones. It's that or nothing else ... we can't stay home all the time on weekends just splittin' and stackin' wood or clumpin' around in garden."

Well, you can be sure that Conrad's fourth and fifth attempts didn't come anywhere close to Bunny's twenty-two skips.

Just Keep Going North..

"You're a pretty good stone-skipper, Aunt Bunny," said Trixie, her ten-year-old niece. "Geez, I wish I could skip as good as you do. When are you gonna' teach me how you do it? I'd sure like to be able to beat those sixth grade boys back home, 'cause they always laugh at us girls and make fun at how we throw. You're really good, though. Wow, twenty-two skips. I bet that's a record!"

Needless to say, Conrad and Bunny later talked about the day's events. Conrad was a bit sore that Bunny didn't stay out of the stone-skipping stuff. He felt she could have said she didn't want to skip stones ... maybe she could have said it was destroying the beach or something like that. Bunny cooled things down by admitting that it was just luck and that she was sure she couldn't do it again in a million years. And, besides her relatives were leaving in the morning and they'd forget all about it.

Conrad wasn't so sure. He knew that Hank, her brother, was sure to bring it up when he got a chance, which is exactly what he did. He came right out at the breakfast table the next morning and asked Conrad: "How does it feel to have your wife beat you at stone-skipping, big guy, there, Conrad?"

"Well, *Heinrich*" (Hank hated that name and Conrad knew it), replied Conrad, "if I had a choice of losing to a "cheese-head" like you or a sport like my wife, I'd lose to her every time just to get a reaction outta' you. And, by the way, there, *Heinrich*, you still want that picture framed of that perch you caught on Saturday? That's a beaut! All seven inches of it, real nice scales. You don't see many fish like that these days, unless somebody from Racine is lucky enough to catch one. Whad'ja use ... one of those Boopsy-Whoppers, or was it your favor-rite Swizzle-Stick that snagged that monster?"

Things were a bit tense at the Johannson breakfast table for a few seconds, even the aloe plants cringed under the pressure of this inter-family rivalry game. But such discourse is par for the course after engaging in minor summer sports in Duluth. So, remember, be careful with whom and how you fish or pluff if you want to survive the summer.

Chapter seven

Water's Not Supposed To Have Holes In It

For most Duluthians, time and events occur mainly in terms of yesterday, a while back and a long time ago, sometime today, and maybe tomorrow. It doesn't pay to keep track of time accurately once you're on the merry-go-round of life in Duluth.

For much of this week and for a while back now, the cloud cover has been a deep gray, hinting at the possibility of one more six- to eight-inch snowfall, but it failed to materialize. It was cold, if twenty-two below zero is not exactly what you like. But, it's the snow that matters more.

The absence of a regular snowfall depresses Duluthians, especially the skiers, the merchants, and the elderly. Snowfall gives them something to talk about in a relative comparative sense, like how much it used to snow a long time ago, the great blizzard of 1934, 1937, 1942, 1958 - 1964, 1973, and so forth, Mostly, long-term Duluthians still talk about how hard it was giving up those studded tires, how winter equipment sales haven't gotten any better even with those snow-blowers, and how that salt compound used on the city's streets corrodes those foreign cars. Snow gives Duluthians something to talk about, in addition to "what is it gonna' be like tomorrow."

Duluthians have a dependency relationship with snow. If enough of the right kind of snow doesn't fall, that's not good. For example, experiencing snow, and lots of it, is seen as a way to remove the effects of sin, kind of like going to purgatory in this life so a person can be prepared for the cold and biting wind when the "real thing" happens. For the most part, Duluth Catholics know that purgatory and hell are *cold*; these places could never be a place of great heat. That's absolutely unthinkable. This idea is drummed into Duluth youngsters as part of cold-hearted regional theology, which in later life becomes one of the motives prompting early out-migration to fairer climates. You won't find Duluth high school graduates wanting to migrate to Upper Michigan, northern Wisconsin, or even North Dakota, once they've had a taste of warmth year-round.

Just Keep Going North..

Even some very progressive Lutherans and a fair number of fundamentalists from the Head-O-The-Lakes become a bit skeptical of the exact temperature of any afterlife place; anything warm would be a pleasant relief from Northland winters.

This topic has been discussed, of course, by the Duluth Council of Clergy. The old-time pastors, while they smile and don't say much, are personally convinced that hell is not some super-heated, Caribbean or Mediterranean punishment concept. They won't come right out and say it, but they get more mileage from sermons that strike terror into parishioners by suggesting that the road to hell resembles 16th Avenue East after a blizzard; that hell is cold, really cold, with a windchill of minus fifty. It doesn't have to be Bible-based to convince Duluthians. After all, the expression, "It's cold as hell," originated right here in Duluth, not Alaska or Canada. Even tourists use this local phrase when attempting to swim in Lake Superior in July.

*   *   *

But, as I was saying, when the cold is accompanied by snow, like it usually is, Duluthians have something to talk about. Snow accumulation generally just happens naturally in Duluth, although the frequency and volume are often quite unnatural. Most Duluthians believe there has to be some ulterior motive behind snowfall that has so far escaped their detection. (Some have even gone so far as to blame those down-state legislators for tampering with the weather, or even blaming the interruptions in regular snowfall on New Age thinking brought in by tourists.)

However, things like snow accumulation simply don't happen by themselves. Something has to cause it, and the way to bring it under control is to tax it. Everybody knows that life in Duluth is taxing; taxing everything possible achieves a high level of social compliance. So, why not apply the tax idea to the physical world to achieve the same degree of regularity and conformity?

Snowfall is one of the few things the city has been studying extensively, especially from all the tax angles. Those unassigned junior attorneys down in the city's legal office have just about figured out a way to tax snow accumulation, but they're pretty closemouthed about such things. I suppose if somebody could prove to them that

Just Keep Going North...

snowfall was absolutely natural, it might undercut their legal position and force them into a strict constitutional position. In any event, the city is working closely on snowfall issues in cooperation with the Western Lakes Sanitary District. After all, it stands to reason that somebody ought to pay for that snow falling, then melting and running into the streets, and creating all those potholes in the spring. So, a property owner's tax on snow accumulation is not mere idle speculation.

Always ahead of the game, the Mayor has even proposed creating a new unit in the City Tax Department so the city could collect snowfall taxes right after a hefty snow — door-to-door. That idea should put a smile on many faces in Duluth, because it's that kind of economic thinking and pursuit of opportunity that Duluthians enjoy most, almost as much as figuring out how to avoid paying such a tax.

Needless to say, when the *Minneapolis Star & Tribune* starts printing pictures of five-foot embankments on Duluth's downtown streets, well, that really gets to the Duluth Tourist Bureau, who in turn, gets to the Public Works Department. Some down-state clique, mostly from St. Paul and Minneapolis, enjoys sticking it to Duluth, both in the newspapers and on TV. Given a chance, they enjoy depicting Duluth as if it were some outpost, some scruffy, old-fashioned, and un-progressive backwater port. (And, who are these Twin Citians to talk? ... what with all their wealth, power, and vitality?) Everybody knows Duluth is not exactly a hotbed of indigenous innovators. Everybody knows that! Everybody here knows that Duluth's economic future is entirely tied to getting state funding for the zoo. But, Duluthians don't like to be reminded of their foibles, anymore than Twin Citians relish being teased for their prosperity, intense competition, and drive, even if the reminder resembles reality, much less fact.

So, the Public Works Department had its truck with the snowbank crusher and vacuum-toss moving down Superior Street. The supervisor would have sent the other three snow-removal trucks down to help out, but the repair work on them seemed to be taking a bit longer than expected — about three months longer. It gets to be rather noisy on Superior Street as these snow-removal trucks grind up the icy embankments — but the noise makes up for the lack of shoppers and workers in the downtown area, sort of creating signs of life.

Just Keep Going North..

Once removed, all that snow, ice, and salt-sand mixture is dumped onto city-owned land, down by the bay. No one paid much attention to this practice until some of the local environmentalists started saying this wasn't right, that it could create a problem in later years.

Sure enough, the City Planning Agency tackled that problem, along with the Lake Superior Water Research Lab. According to their results, there could be a real saltwater inland sea by the year 2047 if the city keeps dumping all that salt in the bay.

No problem, though. City Planning turned around and got a grant to study the feasibility of a salt extraction plant, which would go a long way toward alleviating the salt-deposition problem. The NE Minnesota Economic Development Agency got wind of the inland saltwater sea prediction and secured a grant from the Greater Minnesota Corporation to undertake a feasibility study of marine aquaculture, such as raising lobsters, shrimp, and oysters. Sure enough, there's real economic opportunity and potential at the Head-O-The-Lakes, if a person knows how to figure out where it is and how to capitalize on it. That's the real meaning of self-initiative and technical ingenuity in this neck of the woods, where everybody is eager to get their rightful share.

So, while the environmentalists feel slightly put off, they are the first to admit that Duluth really knows how to manage its ecology with maximum resource expenditure, with micro-economic returns in mind.

You have to give those planners and economic developers credit for dreaming up and tapping into those problems and then devising such creative solutions that further unlikely problems naturally multiply and expand opportunities. It's called "regional idea-generation and adaptive technology transfer." It's as close to a perpetual motion concept as will likely ever be achieved in Duluth, and it's all fueled by devising imaginary problems that come true with a little bit of help in the right direction.

There's a practical side to some of these concerns that many down-staters and out-staters probably don't even know about. Look what happened when the city was told it had to start filtering out the asbestos fibers from the city water supply out there at the pumping station.

The real concern was about what to put back into the water to fill the space previously occupied by the asbestos fibers. After all, water is supposed to be complete; it isn't supposed to have holes in it; that wouldn't be proper water, as least as Duluthians know it. And, further, maybe there was something else unintentionally lost by removing those asbestos fibers, despite what the health officials had to say.

So, in the heat of this discussion, a consultant came to town to talk at one of those town "idea-generation" and issue sessions. The topic had to do with asbestos fiber removal and stopping some mining operation up the North Shore from dumping tailings into Lake Superior. Smart as a whip, even anticipating what would happen when asbestos fibers were taken out of city water, she suggested that "it wasn't the asbestos fibers in the water that mattered, but it was the 'moral fiber' in the people."

That idea captivated a lot of folks, even some of the water scientists and top-notch U.M.-D. types. (University of Minnesota - Duluth: its first acronym was D.- U.M., which was changed for obvious reasons.)

The idea was unexpectedly simple and compelling; it could not be overlooked. Take out the asbestos fibers and put something in that Duluthians really needed.

Some of the other ideas for filling the holes in the water, for bringing it back up to par, were really absurd. Imagine, some scientists talked about putting in some ingredient (like an unnamed sexual hormone) to attract tourists and put some zip into the populace. That idea was rejected, but not until the moral fiber idea was equally exhausted. Some $225,000 later, it was determined that although the idea of putting moral fiber into Duluth's drinking water was sound, it appeared that the shelf-life, stability, and taste of moral fiber — especially at normal concentrations — argued against further pilot work. The study also concluded that certain population sectors developed severe reactions to the experimental formulations of moral fiber additives, including most Duluth politicians, Tourist Bureau and City Legal Department personnel, plus many persons of high standing in Duluth's power structure. Lacking any reasonable explanation for the curious physical reaction to the additive, further study was called for. The grant proposal, however, was rejected by the National Institutes of Mental Health, most unwisely.

Chapter eight

The Personalized Fast-Track Sauna & Sunshine Clinic

The Personalized Fast-Track Sauna & Sunshine Clinic opened on Superior Street this week, which, since there aren't many new businesses started in Duluth, will take some explaining. First, the sunshine part should be obvious, since there's practically no sunshine in Duluth from November through April. So, it helps to think of a tanning salon, but not exactly the usual kind of a salon.

By mid-January, Duluthians give real meaning to the term paleface, not that any Native Americans residing in Duluth would use such a pejorative term of reference when more convenient terms are customary in polite Annishinabe society. Overall, then, any little bit of sunshine that could be brought to Duluth would be welcome, and it wouldn't have to be for the tourists, either, just mainly for the native Duluthians themselves.

The sauna part is a bit more complicated, even if you think you're familiar with the basic idea of a sauna. Why? Because in the hands of the Jarvimaki brothers, the old-fashioned idea of Finnish sauna took a mighty leap forward in design and technology.

Since it's unlikely you know the Jarvimaki brothers, it'll hurt to get filled in a bit. First, there's Waino, he's the older of the two, and Victor, and he's the taller one. Actually, most people call Waino, Wayne, except for the commercial loan officer down at the First National Bank on Superior Street. Nobody except his mother calls Victor, Victor; it's always been just Vic. Anyway, these brothers got their heads together and planned out the "dream, fast-service sauna" system. It took them close to six months, and they did a lot of designing and scheming to get things in place.

For starters, you have to understand that with all those businesses leaving downtown Duluth, space was no problem. There was plenty of prime real estate, at street level, just begging to be occupied. And, besides, there was plenty of steam, since most of downtown Duluth is steam-heated by the Duluth Steam Corporation (except for the Chamber of Commerce offices, the DFL regional headquarters, and the porno shops, because those places seem to

Just Keep Going North..

generate enough heat all by themselves). And if you have steam, you're just a step away from a hot sauna, and Vic factored all that into the site plan. After all, he used to be a pipe-fitter until all that "asbestos stuff" cut off his business.

Wayne Jarvimaki used to own the concessions and rides down at the end of Park Point a long time back, including the Ferris wheel, the merry-go-round, the kiddie train, and the karmel korn stand. But, when the city refused to extend his operating permit, Wayne sold off some of the amusement rides and kept the rest. He had a collection of amusement ride parts, merry-go-round horses, old kiddie train rails, and Lord knows what else in his double garage over on 48th Avenue West.

So, the brothers wanted to get back into business in the worst way, and this personalized fast-track sauna and sunshine clinic idea sounded pretty good to them. It even sounded feasible to the commercial loan officer over at First Bank, on Superior Street, as do most ideas when expressed by Duluthians with carefully chosen words, rehearsal, and modest enthusiasm.

It was no problem for the Jarvimaki's to rent the first floor of Wahl's old department store, right down there on Superior Street, between 2nd and 3rd Avenue West, upper side of the street. They did some remodelling and put in the necessary equipment.

The basic idea was that customers would enter into a lounge area, pay their money, and walk through a small forest of pine-scented, plastic balsam trees, palm trees, birch saplings, with some stuffed animals, including deer, bison, and Vic's stuffed polar bear from his trip to the Northwest Territories. This was to create the right kind of atmosphere, a solid North Country ambience.

Each customer would step into a self-enclosed, plastic sauna bubble, an eight-by-six-foot, egg-shaped vehicle, with built-in controls and hoses bringing steam heat to a radiator-like contraption (of Wayne's design) located in the floor, a built-in shower, overhead tanning lights, and a mood couch. It took a lot of imagination and hard work to design those sauna units. The sauna bubbles would follow the tracks, salvaged from the kiddie train, along the floor, giving the customers a twenty-five-minute ride. Complete privacy was assured, so the customer could disrobe, lounge in the authentic Finnish towels, and tan or not tan, all for $7.95.

Just Keep Going North..

This sauna was just the thing for the downtown crowd who wanted a "quickie" sauna. And, just imagine, this was in Wahl's old department store. Nobody ever went into Wahl's unless they wanted Wahl's exclusive label. This was special; the aromas from Wahl's perfume department still lingered throughout the first floor. It brought back those good feelings and memories that Wayne and Vic counted on, like when the customers as children first visited Wahl's Department Store during the holidays.

Sooner than expected, a good number of things fell into place for the adventuresome Jarvimaki brothers. Yet, being healthy skeptics, as many Finnish people are prone to be, they tested the whole system from start to finish. The electrical work was contracted out. The steam-heat lines were easily hooked up to the sauna bubbles from a pivoting center steam source. And, on the inside of each of those sauna bubbles, there were complete diagrams for just about every function it could provide. The instrument panels were strictly space age. Victor liked the "Star Trek" image it conveyed; the adhesive-backed, imitation-walnut, shelf paper looked great along the instrument panels. Victor's wife, Debbie, had done the murals along the walls in each sauna bubble, some showing North Country scenes, while others were more flamingo-style art deco. Those four years she spent at the Duluth Art Institute were finally paying off.

On the Personalized Fast-Track Sauna & Sunshine Clinic's first day of business, the Mayor stopped by, but declined to take a free sauna. He thought, as do most Duluth mayors, just keeping his job was a big enough sweat. Everyone laughed at that comment.

Flowers were provided by some of the "ladies" from over at the Oneota Bar, down by the aerial bridge, while the co-owners bought a few cakes from the European Bakery, over on 1st Street. There was free coffee, too, with a regular twenty-six cup coffee-maker purchased just the day before. And, things went ahead pretty much on schedule. Everything looked good.

"Very smooth, very nice," commented Eunice Bergstrom, who'd won a free ticket, adding, "and its a positive addition to Duluth's downtown recovery, a long-needed recreational and mental health service which everyone should consider."

Eunice is running for the School Board and hoped the city's media hounds would pick up on her comments. That's why she went down there in the first place; it wasn't the free ticket. Eunice hasn't

Just Keep Going North..

been in a sauna since she was nineteen. That was her first and last sauna, but I have that only on the word of one of the neighbors.

On Friday, things really heated up. By 11:00 a.m. nearly twenty-four of those sauna units were in use, sometimes carrying two, or even three, people. A few of the tourists coming out looked like parboiled salmon, but then tourists in Duluth hardly ever know what to expect. They just pay, smile, and say they had a great time. The curious thing is that they hardly ever come back, and that's why the Duluth Tourist Bureau has to be so vigilant in identifying new tourist sources. (The Bureau is planning a major ad campaign down in Lima, Peru; Ohio, and Montana.)

Anyway, right before noon, it seems those old kiddie railroad tracks that Wayne had bolted to the floor boards to create the conveyor system, well, something started to get to them. I guess those old floor boards couldn't take the stress. Those kiddie railroad tracks began to spread out, to expand, and the bolts started to pop, crack, and then the floor boards began to heave and twist. About that time, those plastic self-enclosed sauna units — with the one-way plastic "peek-out" window on the top — broke loose and started spinning and rolling toward the front of the building.

It wasn't long before those thirty-five-foot steam hoses tore loose and started whipping and snaking around the floor like you couldn't imagine. It got pretty hot and steamy in a hurry, right there in old Wahl's Department Store, first floor, where nothing but proper Duluth decorum was ever seen in more than sixty years.

Well, those sauna units started to gain momentum as they fell and slid off those tracks, rolling and careening around. Weighing close to 1,000 pounds each, they broke right through the plastic North Country jungle, rolled past the cashier, crashed through the glass windows in Wahl's old storefront, and propelled themselves clear out onto the sidewalk and the street, where the Public Works truck was sucking up snowbanks. Yup, it all took place in a matter of seconds, right there on the north side of Superior Street.

The looks on the faces of those Public Works people defied description, as those sauna bubbles rolled out onto Superior Street. It was like someone had put a bucket of live smelt in their waders. They moved faster than they'd ever done, even at quitting time.

It was a sight to behold. Those sauna bubbles rolling around the sidewalk, falling into the street, while those Public Works people

Just Keep Going North..

tried to get out of their way. People came racing down Superior Street, cars tooted and braked, and even the West-End-bound bus stopped. Inside, the Jarvimaki brothers were dashing around trying to find the steam valve, while dodging steam lines. It was really getting hot, but those Jarvimaki's have a great sense of humor; they kept on smiling the whole time.

You can be certain there was no racing or dashing of people out of those plastic sauna bubbles, and, maybe not just because of the temperature altogether.

The Public Works site supervisor tried to get out of the cab of his truck, but the door was held tight by one of those sauna bubbles. He went into shock and was the first victim taken to St. Mary's Trauma Center.

Order was restored, more or less, after the downtown squad car arrived, although it took a world of doing to coax those people out of those sauna units ... what with the *NooStribune* photographer there and all.

There is a closed sign hanging on the door to the Personalized Fast-Track Sauna & Sunshine Clinic now. Nobody seems to know whether it will re-open or not. I suppose there's a moral here someplace and it has to do with "brain-storming" technology, design layout, and rented facilities. But, I think it has more to do with old floor boards, warped tracks, and wanting to get into business in the worst possible way.

If you see some curious egg-shaped structures posing as new rides at the Duluth Zoo this summer, it's probably those Jarvimaki brothers at it again, doing what they know best, providing amusement.

You might even meet the Jarvimaki brothers, which would be more fun than you deserve!

Chapter nine

It Could Happen

This past week turned out to have eight days in it, at least for some Duluthians. Things like that can happen in Duluth, though they're rare. It seems the A & B Print Shop made a mistake in the layout of their "give-away" appointment calendars, resulting in two January twenty-fifth's. Of course, this was reported in the Duluth *Grudgeteer*, whose editor had sent out a reporter to find out how the extra day had affected people.

Some Duluthians reported that they were really quite upset about the matter, since they weren't exactly able to figure out which day really was the twenty-fifth, and nobody in city hall, the library, or at 911 was able to help them. Others felt a bit cheated by losing a whole extra day. But, for the great majority of Duluthians, for those who merely mutter about the windchill as they walk up Lake Avenue, it didn't really matter. It doesn't pay to give too much attention to one day over another; they're all pretty much the same, maybe even more so in the winter.

Well, the A & B Print Shop ran an ad apologizing for any inconvenience its calendar caused, but that didn't exactly sit right with some people. In fact, people at the barbershops, the bakeries, the gas stations, and a few other places that regularly buy these give-away calendars from the A & B Print Shop, thought that maybe, just maybe, this thing could happen again. And that was worrisome.

People in Duluth come to count on things like the calendar being right. If a person has to worry about whether it will be right next month, or the month after that, well, this kind of worry can erode your sense of quality of life from the bottom up. So people let it be known that they were going to check those calendars more carefully in the future, even if they were free.

The best idea came from one of the neighbors who noted that the mistake probably occurred because those calendars were given out free, adding that if you had to pay for them, these kinds of mistakes wouldn't happen. And, I suppose there's a curious logic to that, because everyone in Duluth knows you get exactly what you pay for, including mistakes. That's just practical quality manage-

Just Keep Going North..

ment. As Duluthians learned once more, it pays to be more sensitive to hidden costs in things, especially when the newspaper editor starts giving out fancy mathematical formulas, such as free equals negative costs plus hidden costs.

The econometric thinking rampant in Duluth staggers most down-state types, especially the down-state legislators. Imagine: the Duluth legislative team asking the Minnesota House to pay back for minerals already removed from northern Minnesota, as part of economic re-development. As one rural down-state legislator put it, "How in the world can these northern legislators think we would be gullible enough to give them tax money for minerals already extracted? If it were in my power, I'd give 'em back all their iron ore and tell 'em to fill up those mines and start over." Those kind of sentiments certainly fuel regional pride in "extraction politics and economics."

Chapter ten

Now, Isn't That Really Something

It all began when Thelma Nordstrand said she was going to retire. Thelma had been the head dietitian, nutritionist, and food service director of the School District for thirty-four years, before which she'd been a school nurse and later district nursing supervisor. I guess she got into nutrition because she felt students kept mixing up the Big Six with the Top Ten. And that's understandable, since some people confuse minerals with the Rolling Stones and breakfast cereals with vitamins.

Thelma was a very dedicated person; when she put her heart into a job, it stayed there. There was really nobody who could dislodge her from Food Service operations. They tried, but she stayed put, and so did her notions of nutrition and menus.

Yet with time, and it did take time — almost three superintendents came and left — Thelma's retirement was inevitable.

So, she submitted her resignation and the District held a going-away party, actually a potluck dinner, out at the picnic pavilion at Lester Park. Thelma didn't want anything fancy and she didn't think she'd enjoy herself down at Fitgers or one of those "high-ticket" restaurants down on Superior Street.

The dinner plans were set. At around 5:30, on a somewhat chilly June 10, about eight cars pulled into the Lester Park parking lot, at just about the same time that the fog started to creep up from the lake. It was convenient somehow to locate those city parks close by Lake Superior in the old days, because this way the horses didn't have to haul up those hills. But this means that Duluth city parks are subject to fog attacks without warning. Of course the fog holds the mosquitoes and gnats down a bit, but not much; Duluth's insect life has been given permanent refuge in city parks, in exchange for which they're regarded as year-round residents for census and tax purposes.

The fog wasn't actually that bad since a person could still see the outlines of the cars from the picnic pavilion, about seventy-five feet away. Most Duluthians are able to live with fog; they have to since there's no choice in the matter. But when the fog turns to mist,

Just Keep Going North..

to that light misty rain that everyone knows can linger all night around the lake, well, it makes a person stop and think: "I wouldn't be here if it weren't for Thelma, and this can't last forever."

When the fire in the concrete fireplace turns to a gray, smoky smudge, you know Duluthians are smiling if they have a purpose, being good-natured on the outside, but not for long.

Mel Schmidt, the assistant superintendent, hurried things up a bit. He politely refused third helpings, swished down his fourth cup of ARCO coffee, and headed for his car. He returned, of course, carrying what these staffers and teachers knew would signal the climax of the party — the gift-giving time.

You can be sure Thelma not only got a few gifts, but she got the right kind of gifts. Duluthians don't tend to go in for those big, splashy, trendy retirement gifts, like shuffleboard sets, fish smokers, or yogurt-makers. They try to pick out gifts that are personal, that have a lot of significance behind them, which means these gifts fall somewhere between foundation garments and linens, if you know the layout in the Glass Block Department Store, second floor.

Mel made the presentations on behalf of the District. There was an imitation oak plaque bearing a brass-coated plate, with the words:

THELMA NORRSTRAND

For

Outstanding

Service

in

Food Service

Mel noted the misspelling of Thelma's last name and said he'd have that taken care of it — it was either that or she could change the spelling of her last name. Mel has a sense of humor that takes some getting used to. Not unlike many professional educators, he's not known for his one-liners; rather, Mel has a gift for spinning four sentences into a forty-five-minute parable, complete with a cast of thousands, the weather forecast, and a dash of pathos. Mel's stories rarely have a punch line. They appear to have some moral buried deep inside them, or so Mel's listeners suspect. Mel waits for a while

Just Keep Going North..

after telling a story and then nudges the listener with the question: "Hey, wha'dja think of that!? Isn't that something!?"

It's better to agree with Mel right off, otherwise he'll take another forty minutes to explain the key ideas. And don't let Mel tell his stories near a blackboard because he has this tendency to outline main points as he's relating the story. Most students would rather have four hours of detention than listen to one of Mr. Schmidt's stories about real life out there — beyond and within the socio-ethical parameters of Duluth.

The Food Service staff gave Thelma a fondue set, which included eight silver fondue forks, six hand-edged napkins, and a tablecloth, plus a can of fondue fuel, all very nicely gift-wrapped.

Someone came up with the idea of framing Thelma's first and last school lunch menus, which was thoughtful and showed that things hadn't really changed that much over thirty-four years.

Last, there was *the envelope*. Every retiree from the Duluth School District expects to get the envelope. It contains a life-time subscription to *Adventures in Retirement*, a farewell card, and the first of many hoped-for retirement checks.

Thelma smiled and thanked everyone. And that was about it. No tears, no hugs, just plain, heartfelt thanks, simple good-byes, and best wishes.

The leftovers and hot-dish plates were packed up faster than usual, plastic cups and other recyclables stashed away. It didn't take more than ten minutes for the pavilion to be emptied.

Standing in the mist, her hair-net beaded with glistening raindrops, Thelma supervised the cleanup operation. As the guest of honor, it was her last task to indicate that the tables and area looked OK to her. And, that was it. The next day, Thelma and her sister left for Eureka, California, where they had bought a condo. Duluth was now a fading memory in a long chain of memories in a long life of hot lunches and menu planning.

Fortunately for him, Thelma's successor was hired before she left. In fact, she handpicked him. She liked John immediately; yes, John Magnusson was her clear choice as the right candidate for her old job. Not only did he have solid credentials, but with a name like Magnusson, he'd fit right in with the Duluth crowd.

Just Keep Going North..

Actually, John was from Detroit. It seems some Scandinavians just didn't have the staying power to get all the way to the Head-O-The Lakes. Many of those Scandinavian pioneers just sort of rested along the way as they looked for the fabled Viking House made of Smoked Herring, Lefsa, and Silta in the midst of the Opdahl Forest; the longer they rested and looked, the harder it was to keep going north. That's why there are pockets of Scandinavians all along the lower Midwest, just filled with people who quit the great trek northward. Most of these people know the Promised Land is somewhere up by Lake Superior, near Duluth, maybe even in Duluth. At least once or twice in their lifetime they plan and make a pilgrimage northwards, seeking to find out what it was that prompted their grandparents to want to come here in the first place.

After driving from somewhere south to Duluth with the whole family, walking around a bit, photographing the aerial bridge, and sticking a toe in Lake Superior, someone in the party is bound to say something like: "Geez, just imagine ... we could have wound up here!" This is followed by a thoughtful pause, after which the general response is: "Let's go! I'm freeeezing! The lake is too cold for wading, and the kids want something to eat. If you want to see more of this place, go ahead. Just take me and the kids back to the motel."

It's not easy for these Viking descendants from gentler climes to get with the Duluth spirit. But, then, it's hard spiritually to appreciate Duluth when your teeth are chattering and a flock of seagulls is hovering and screeching overhead. Maybe that's why Duluth is less of a place for some people, and more of a state of mind.

Thelma Nordstrand knew that, and she knew it wouldn't be easy breaking in a new person, not in a job she had molded to her own likes and personality. But, then, she'd just have to do her best in the time available.

John Magnusson was rather easygoing. And, no doubt about it, he was also very thorough-going. He asked more direct questions than an English teacher enrolled in a mandatory in-service course on transformational grammar. He was full of questions. You have to understand that John's background included food service management, in addition to a degree program in nutrition. He was extremely conscientious, some might say even zealous, but that seems to go with a background in food service operations management these days.

Just Keep Going North..

But it was mostly the numbers that interested him, numbers like those on the monthly inventories and revenues, numbers on staffing and payroll. Numbers were the part of the job Thelma liked least. True, she knew about those numbers, but she never bothered with them much. She just signed off on reports and sent them to accounts payable. Thelma's numbers management almost drove the District food service accountant to the brink.

Tim Knudsen, the food service accountant, was never able to discuss revenues, order quantities, much less food costs, with Thelma. She'd just clam up and say she was too busy, that it was his job to keep the numbers in place, and that was it. When Thelma decided not to talk about something, it was pointless to even ask why. Of course, there was the one time when she told Mr. Knudsen what he could with all his numbers, and that episode rather chilled relations between them. It had to do with Thelma ordering too many hot-dog buns for the teacher orientation program.

So, Mr. Knudsen was the last person Thelma acquainted John with, figuring he could blaze his own trail to the food service account manager's desk. And, Mr. Knudsen in turn was positively elated that Thelma was leaving, not that he said anything one way or the other. Maybe, just maybe, this new person could make some sense out of what went on in food services.

Needless to say, John spent the better part of the summer months getting acquainted with the staff at the various schools, visiting with Tim Knudsen, and going over the past year's figures. There was a lot to learn. He even talked to the parent's subcommittee on food and menu planning. To John, school meals were as important as geography, as books or math. Just try mentally getting to Oslo or visualizing a solid geometry problem on an empty stomach, was what he told that parent group. They agreed it was a difficult job. They even opened up about the food habits of their kids, indicating they didn't exactly know what most kids ate, except that things seemed to vanish regularly from their refrigerators. The parents hoped John could nutritionally balance out what they seemed unable to supply. It would be fair to say that John had those parents eating out of his hands at the end of that session. He'd convinced them all right that good sound meals were in the works for the District.

By late August, John had just about completed his review. His analysis showed that Thelma had done a pretty good job at

Just Keep Going North..

creating new food combinations, some of which he'd never heard of before, like pita bread stuffed with tuna-fish salad and black olives, and a variety of pizza with a shredded chow-mein noodle and cheddar topping.

He was ready to give his interim report and plan to the assistant superintendent, Mel Schmidt. Schmidt's cluster of duties included overseeing food service, counseling and discipline, faculty promotion and tenure, along with elementary curriculum affairs. This is by no means an unusual combination of duties in the Duluth District if you remember that tasks are assigned by lottery. Mel had even swapped driver education on the District's "swap-a-job" day to get food service operations.

John was prepared to tell Mel that it seemed some of the management practices in the past were handicapped by modest planning, or even the absence of planning. Of course, he didn't want to put any blame on Thelma's efforts, which in the main were pretty good. He wanted to stress that his sense of the job meant to manage, really manage, all operations more closely, especially the planning and revenue side. John had readied a twenty-two-page report, which included some key recommendations, charts, tables, and many numbers. If you weighed that report, the numbers would have come out far ahead of the letters.

The meeting between John Magnusson and Mel Schmidt would have been quite profitable, were it not for the fact that on that very morning Mel had undergone one of those critical mid-career experiences associated with educational administration; he had been turned down for the job of superintendent over at Proctor. His heart had been set on that job, so his mind was not really on food service matters. In fact, only five minutes into John's presentation, Mel started to tell John a story.

Well, you can be sure that John listened attentively, nodded where appropriate, searched for the message, and even encouraged Mel with a few chuckles. Mel rambled on, backtracked a few times, went over fifteen years of administrative experience, and wound up that story by taking John mentally right down to the edge of Lake Superior in the middle of a blizzard, to something that happened back in 1984 sometime. He paused, looked at John, and said, "Wha'dja think of that!? Isn't that something!?"

John could only agree. Yep, that really was something, but he didn't have the vaguest idea what it was or what it meant.

Mel confided, "Listen, John, you continue doing things pretty much the way Thelma used to do, and things should be fine. I know I can count on you. I'll read your report later, and we'll cook up some recommendations to send over to the School Board for one of their fall meetings. Let me know if you run into any bad apples."

True, outsiders might think the management style and the outcome of that meeting were exaggerated. But, like most things in Duluth, there's often a deeper, more subtle, set of meanings to matters. So, take my word for it, things in Duluth aren't always what they seem — they're often a silk purse cleverly disguised as a sow's ear.

In Duluth, as down-staters have learned through costly experience, there are two kinds of meetings: High Meetings and Low Meetings. John didn't know about Duluth meeting styles; he thought his meeting with Mel was to be informative.

Yet, as every Duluthian knows, you can't hold a High Meeting — the kind John thought he was getting into and for which he'd prepared his report — with just two people. And, you can't expect a Low Meeting to produce any sure results. These are simply things people have to learn, apply, and cultivate as part of mastering the Duluth management style. John was learning, and it sure wasn't like anything they'd taught him over at Wayne State.

Well, with all the encouragement given by Mel Schmidt, John plunged into the school year. He started to monitor revenues, food unit sales by day and week, by building, staffing, and food orders. He was starting to get a fairly good feel for things. And, even Tim Knudsen told him it certainly was a pleasure to work with him. Of course, Tim did his best to keep John up to his eyeballs in numbers. Tim figured that sooner or later John would discover what he'd been trying to tell anyone who would listen. It seems Tim Knudsen wasn't exactly high in the District's pecking order, but he sure knew his beans as most bean-counters do.

By mid-October, John got the distinct feeling that something was wrong. He studied those school food units reported and there were simply too few students using the food service. Even when the very best menu items of the week were offered, the numbers of students dropped off. He re-examined the food preference surveys.

Just Keep Going North..

True enough, those best menus were chasing demand, but student demand seemed to have its own dynamics. It was as if some sinister factor was behind all this. He clearly didn't have the answers, but he knew he had to find out what was gong on. It seemed to boil down to two simple facts: there was too much wastage, and yet there was also unaccounted for revenue.

The rest of October didn't improve the facts or the situation either. Revenues dipped, then increased, and finally vanished somewhere into November's accounts.

There was only one thing to do. Call a staff meeting. And, that's what John did. He sent a memo out requesting that all the building food supervisors attend a meeting on November 14, adding that there were a number of items he wanted to review with the entire staff.

Well, it's time you learned more about meetings in Duluth, or the rest of the story will seem like Mel had a hand in it. In Duluth, there are only two reasons for calling a High Meeting: one, because a problem has reached crisis proportions and it's time to spread blame and guilt around to make the problem go away, or two, to tell people exactly what's going to happen to them, how and when, but not why.

Duluthians know it is completely inappropriate in meetings to tell people *why*. It's also very bad form to answer why questions in public meetings if everyone there is a Duluthian; exceptions might be made if an outsider is present, but then the outsider is taken aside and told why. Why do things take this course? The answer is simple: in Duluth everybody knows why a High Meeting is called and if they don't they shouldn't be there.

It's more important to let Duluthians figure out why questions for themselves. Why questions are the button that activates the superego, Head-O-The Lakes syndromes, and complexes, and drive the archetypes in the Duluth personality. Wonderment and speculation feed the inner psyche of Duluthians, regardless of how well placed they might be, how old, or even how many advanced degrees they hold.

The preoccupation of Duluthians with self-devised and other imposed why questions is so pervasive, unremitting and all-encompassing, it can be equated to a virtual out-of-body, out-of-mind, episode, as related by Sufi mystics and ice-fishing addicts.

Just Keep Going North..

So, if not allowed to speculate about why questions, including the anxiety they provoke, Duluthians lose their drive, their get up and go, their ability to make up stories, and their power to explain matters to themselves.

It's far better to let Duluthians fabricate their own answers to why questions than to feed their doubts about anything that remotely resembles alternatives or truth; in Duluth, truth is a personal, subjective position usually triggered by a degree of guilt about one's inability to explain life and events in Duluth, much less elsewhere; truth is what other people want to convince you of, and Duluthians won't have much to do with that kind of thinking. To the Duluthian, it only matters how and what he or she thinks. The rule is, if you don't know why, you'd better get busy; the only way to see the light is to stick your whole head into the why question.

Perhaps now people from other regions and areas who come to Duluth will realize just how difficult it is to imagine, much less manage, a city like this, to grasp its culture, and survive within its social order, given the turmoil created by why questions.

Anticipating a High Meeting, even thinking about a High Meeting, builds incredible tension. It requires each person to create a complete set of why answers. So, Duluthians will do anything possible to avoid or prevent a High Meeting. This includes making covert attempts to find out in advance who's going to get blamed, or inventing some whopping excuse for not attending.

Yet, High Meetings cannot be postponed; they're as inevitable as the wail of the police siren on Sunday mornings on Woodland Avenue before eight. They are as certain as *Manny's Mailer* in Saturday's mail, but just a bit less certain than death and taxes. The best way to prepare for a High Meeting is to approach it with the same attitude one might bring to an IRS tax review or a traffic court appearance, namely: be quiet, maintain outward dignity, rehearse answers, project intense curiosity about details, and display the confidence of the guilty when the verdict is read.

High Meetings call for protocol and strict observance of procedure. High Meetings are pure theater; ritualized enactments that demonstrate great moral principles to everyone through apt staging of human affairs. A lot of power can be dissipated in a High Meeting; social capital can be wasted on the wrong agenda for the right reasons, and vice versa.

By contrast, Low Meetings are informal; they take place to decide who all gets the blame, how to portion to out, and who the real culprits are. Low Meetings get out opinions and motives and set the stage for High Meetings. Low Meetings occur all the time in staff rooms, at bars after work, even in parking lots. If not networked into either a High or Low Meeting, the best thing to do is to keep off your telephone and wait for the right call.

Low Meetings typically begin when someone says, "Well, I don't know if this is right, but I think we oughta' do something about it ... and here's my idea. Of course, I wanna' hear what you gotta' say, too."

Low Meetings help people to figure out whether or not everyone else is worried about the same why question, or why not. People have to be very careful when Low Meetings start out since it never pays to express one's true feelings right away. That would be rushing matters and spoil all the fun of future Low Meetings. In Duluth, you have to get the timing and sequence of real issues down, or you won't be invited into the power structure.

Of course, John Magnusson didn't have the vaguest idea that Duluthians had such sophisticated and well-orchestrated ideas about meetings. He'd taken a Continuing Education shortcourse in meeting management, back at Wayne State. But either the course was too short or the instructors couldn't have imagined that a competing set of meeting principles had been developed in Duluth. So, he sent out a second reminder of the meeting, and, by that act, everyone knew it was going to be a High Meeting of some sort.

The meeting took place in the conference room down at old Central High School, the present District headquarters. Everyone was curiously early, equipped with notebooks and file folders. There was a minimum of chitchat.

Cory Fastness was appointed temporary recording secretary by John, which prompted Luverne Olsen to suggest that maybe a whole slate of officers — except, quite naturally, a chairperson, might be useful. So a treasurer was nominated, along with a few other titles. Dorothy Adams volunteered to serve as Sergeant-at-Arms, since she was not elected treasurer. The group wasn't certain whether a chaplain was necessary, necessitating a moment of silent delay while the why part of the issue was processed. The importance of getting off on the right foot in a High Meeting cannot be overly stressed, especially if you don't know what's coming later on.

John began the meeting with a review of current menus, using the principle that it's wise to get rid of some trivial things so as to better concentrate on the important few. He moved next to the student/teacher food preference survey, followed by the revenue picture, always asking whether there were any questions.

No one had any questions; no one surely had come up with a personally satisfying answer as to why this meeting was called; *why* was still uppermost in the minds of the people assembled around that big oval table in the conference room.

Then John let go with the real purpose of the meeting. It was this: if he couldn't find a way to reduce stock and staple inventories and improve student use of food services, well, it looked as if there might be some cuts made in staff and supervisory personnel. "It just looks that way," said John. "Are there any questions?"

No questions were posed. There was tension though; swarms of anxiety were collecting at all the Chakra centers and emanating flashing green, red, and yellow rays. The quiet in that room was unworldly. It was so quiet, so tense, you could have heard ants breathing, if there had been any in that room. That's what participants are supposed to feel at a High Meeting; they should have lots of self-contained stress and discomfort. Not even School District coffee and European Bakery cupcakes seemed to alleviate the mounting pressure.

The only collective thought held by those Food Service supervisors was, "Well, when's he going to start blaming people so we can get on with this meeting?"

By this time, Marlys Peterson had stopped her knitting and simply clutched a yellow-orange-brown Afghan patch in her lap, with needles at the ready. Emil Jensen sat straighter than he'd ever sat in one of those contoured conference chairs; Emil had perfected the slouch to the point that it appeared chairs actually adopted his shape, all 260 pounds and his six-foot, four-inch frame. The quiet just went on and no one said anything.

John knew if he broke the tension, it wouldn't be "their meeting" anymore. Ownership of meeting outcomes was one of those shortcourse principles he'd remembered, and he wanted it to

Just Keep Going North..

be their meeting. Instead, it looked as if it was going to be *his* meeting. He didn't want that.

There was no eye contact; everyone was looking at some invisible defect in the table's polished surface about midway between themselves and their neighbor. Emil even started to count wall tiles, which he did whenever subjected to great nervous strain, a survival practice he learned years ago.

Finally, Dorothy Adams scooted forward in her chair and prepared to say the thing that everyone feared. Her motion jarred everyone back to the meeting's real intent. It was time to start dishing out the blame. Time to get what you had coming to you, which is a baseline feeling most Duluthians recognize even before it consciously arrives. This feeling is the prime motivator around here.

In the food service business, there are just three things nobody wants to hear: ptomaine, "What kinda' food is that supposed to be?", and pilferage. And Dorothy had said one of those things right at a High Meeting. That assertiveness course had certainly paid off for her. Yep, she came right out and asked Mr. Magnusson if he thought there was a pilferage problem. Pilferage!

Food thefts. People taking things they weren't supposed to take, like rice, leftover hamburgers, carrot sticks, maybe a piece of apple pie, and probably taking those things home and eating them! That idea hit the group like a Coast Guard cutter purposely ramming into the pier on the ship canal on a calm day. Dorothy waited for some kind of answer from John.

John Magnusson hadn't studied this part of meeting management, called, "what to do when you lose control." He had read about disasters to avoid in meetings, but this coping skill wasn't stressed. He knew meetings weren't supposed to go this way. People were supposed to react, not put him on trial. This was embarrassing. This wasn't how people reached consensus, not by a long shot. This was like a classroom and he was the pupil. Did Marlys' knitting suggest there was a guillotine nearby, maybe in the basement, that maybe they were waiting for him to confess to something? These thoughts zipped through his mind.

"Well, no, I don't know if there is any pilferage or not," began John, "but what do you make of these numbers? What would you do if you were in my position?" His eyes had located that same invisible defect on the polished surface of the table that had previously held the attention of the others.

It seems the meeting ended right there. John didn't even have to say the meeting was over or that it would be rescheduled. Very quietly, with hushed excuses, people just gathered their things and melted through the door. John waited until everyone had left before collecting his own notes and folders and then walked slowly to his office. He was utterly downcast.

This wasn't going to be the job he had hoped for. This situation wasn't going to correct itself, he thought. Duluth as a state of mind was beginning to work on him and he felt terrible, just terribly drained.

Within forty-eight hours there were twelve letters of resignation on his desk. He couldn't believe it. Nearly all the Food Service supervisory staff had sent in their resignations. What was he going to do now? What could he say to that parent's subcommittee? More importantly, what would he say to Mel Schmidt, or the School Board, over this fiasco? Would the teachers boycott the lunchrooms?

Well, it didn't take long before he had conjured up enough worries to fill fourteen working days — probably his last fourteen days in this District — because that's how Duluth gets to you. It demands that you collect worries in a bottomless bag; it triggers the unimaginable and remorselessly redirects guilt if that bag of worries is not filled on time. By Friday, having found the last of those nineteen resignation letters in his pigeonhole mailbox, John also noticed a letter from California, with a postmark from Eureka. A letter from Thelma Nordstrand. He guessed she might have gotten several phone calls from the food service personnel. She was probably writing to tell him to apologize and try to smooth things over. It seemed a bit late for that kind of advice, if that was what she had in mind. But, better to find out what the letter said, because it was clear what he had to do that afternoon.

Dear John:

I hope things are going well for you. To be honest, I got several phone calls from the old Duluth gang. I guess you've got a problem on your hands. The staff doesn't blame you for what happened; in fact, they thought you had been told. I guess it slipped my mind, so let me clear my conscience.

Just Keep Going North..

It seems a few years back we began bringing leftover food down to a few of those missions in Duluth, places where the homeless go. It seems some of these missions couldn't get food-handling licenses because of problems with city ordinances. It was all very complicated, which is typical of how things go in Duluth City Hall. Anyway, what began on a small scale got bigger. A number of homeless and hungry people in Duluth, a lot of families, really needed food. So, the folks in Food Service and the parents organized a grass-roots effort to feed the hungry. The kids would come in, pay for their food, but most often not take any food at all. That's the food we used to feed the hungry, and when we needed to help out more, we took it out of the "special fund." We put the money in a separate account so that grouchy Mr. Tim Knudsen couldn't find it. He'd have reported the whole thing and we would all have been in hot water.

The project helped the people down at the Gospel Mission, the Duluth Refuge, and the West-End Shelter. We even sent food to those old-timers who live in those rather dingy units over the stores on 1st Street. When I left, I'd guess we were feeding close to 400 people off and on. The kids understood what was going on and they thought it was a good way to learn about people and hunger. The parents supported it, too. We just couldn't let everybody in town know about it, because somebody was sure to raise a stink.

Mel Schmidt was in on our secret. Strange, though, he didn't mention anything to you. Maybe he tried, but Mel has a way of getting lost so easily in his own stories.

I hope this has not caused you to feel badly toward me or the Food Service crowd. It would be a shame to see them quit over this misunderstanding. I know you can handle things now. The money is all there, every penny, under account DAHEF — that's District Administrators Holiday & Entertainment Fund. We knew that snoopy Knudsen would never look for it there.

I feel better for sharing this with you. I hope you are still the person I sensed when I recommended your hiring. I've told the people who called that you would want to take the first step. I apologize if this caused you any personal worry or concern.

With kindest regards,

Thelma Nordstrand

So things got rearranged in a hurry with all the Food Service people. It just took a few Low Meetings and things were cooking again. As of late January, Magnusson was given charge of a new food service account, one that has fairly widespread, but unofficial, approval. It's called the Thelma Nordstrand Memorial Food Fund, and it's only been active for two weeks.

It seems retirement was just no match for Thelma. She wasn't going to learn to relax and improvise at her age, and retirement was not the challenge she'd faced for thirty-four years in Food Service. There was quite a turnout at her funeral. Who would have guessed she was seventy-two. Mel Schmidt was asked to give the eulogy, but he declined, except to say a few words at the end of the service about some trust in her will that she had set up to help hungry students and to transport leftovers. The School District attorney was baffled by Thelma's trust, but her request was followed to the letter.

Close to 800 students showed up, and many, many parents, too. You should have heard the stories they told about that woman and how she held things together in Food Service operations all those years. But then, I'd guess everybody had heard them before on the back twining of the grapevine, except for Mel Schmidt. He just listened and listened. And, all he could think of was the time she told him what was really happening with leftover food and the Food Service aid to the hungry. He could scarcely hold back the tears.

The cooperation among those Food Service supervisors is now outstanding. Dorothy Adams was named permanent secretary for the group, just in case another High Meeting is ever called, which now seems quite unlikely, at least that's what the neighbors thought. So, now you know the truth of it and, as Mel would say: "Wha'dja think about that!? Isn't that really something!?"

Chapter eleven

How About Some Free Advice For When It Gets Really Cold

When it gets to be late February, Duluthians anxiously await April, because March is just a rerun of February, give or take a few degrees. Now that it's struck, the *really cold* weather slows people down a bit, but then nobody's certain what the pace in Duluth should be anyway. Things here have a way of pretty much rolling downhill, which follows both the topography and economic outlook most of the time. Ideas that are uphill, sideways, or forward seem to cause deep mental turmoil among Duluthians, as it rightly should for people who insist upon looking at the downside of things as essential for image building.

There's a curious logic in Duluth that defies the half-filled, half-empty bottle model; in Duluth, the issue is whether the bottle is corked or not and whether the bottle is sealed or has been opened. The absence of the conventional dimensions of optimism and pessimism are peculiar to Duluth. They have been replaced by crucial existential issues focused on two questions. Is Duluth what we want it to be because of what we are? Or, is Duluth about to become something else in spite of us? Naturally, these issues are remorseless centerpieces in debates that plague both the DFL and IR parties as they mobilize voter strength and turnout. It turns out that Duluth voters really don't care one way or the other, yet it adds bittersweet spice to the political agenda and wonderment to life in the North Country.

The only forward-looking thing Duluthians look forward to is the first really refreshing blast of cold air and snow as early as November, with any luck at all, or assuredly in December. But, if the *really cold* doesn't come until February, well, that's a long time to wait for what you've got coming to you. People get a bit cranky and out of sorts while waiting for that cold weather to hit.

This year the *really cold* held back until February. This meant that anxieties were stretched to the limits of psychic endurance — people were put to an extraordinary test. As a result, Duluthians have been more ornery than usual, which means it's much harder for them to be their normal introspective, guilt-ridden selves.

Just Keep Going North..

A good cold blast, one of those Alberta Clippers, really tests whether all of those preparations that went into getting the house and car ready really paid off. Duluthians take inordinate, competitive pride in getting ready for winter. They feel cheated if a sin-blasting, cold spell doesn't arrive before Christmas. A really momentous blizzard around Thanksgiving can jolly them right through January, what with all that competitive snow-blowing activity, battery recharging, and street salting aimed at total car destruction.

When the cold weather arrived in February, with most of the snow-birds gone, things just weren't quite right. For example, there was a head-count of twenty-two persons on Superior Street, between 3rd and 4th Avenue West, at noon on Wednesday, which is only actually down two from the height of the tourist season in July.

So, if any of those people downtown are leaning over a fender with the hood open on their car, peering down at the radiator or just staring at the engine block trying to figure out what to do next, you can be certain they're tourists. A tourist, by Duluth definition, is a person who should know better than to come to Duluth, anytime, for any reason, except business, but does so despite obvious warnings; a person who clearly defies common sense for the sake of wanton self-indulgence in uneventfulness, exaggerates personal disappointments, and has a masochistic flair for risk-taking.

Coming to Duluth as a tourist is like winning a lottery to go to Camelot, but winding up at a weekend marriage encounter session for soil scientists. Clearly something is missing, but the obvious takes a few seconds to decipher. As old-time Duluthians put it, a tourist is a person who comes up here, pretty much sees what there's to be seen (because that's about all there is do anyway), and then says to himself: "Yep, I shoulda' stayed back there in Wisconsin at the cabin, bought some cheese, brats, and beer and taken the kids fishing."

Of course, at all other times, except for the brief period between July 2 and 14 — the designated summer season in Duluth — a tourist is a person who got caught in Duluth during the change in the seasons; or, a tourist is one of those gullible down-staters or out-staters who came to Duluth to enjoy something that didn't materialize, like finding an actual mountain for skiing, or groomed snowmobile trails, or some other unattainable winter venture promoted by the Duluth Tourism Bureau. As skiing enthusiasts remark about their adventures to Duluth, "Well, it helps to have the

Just Keep Going North..

'spirit,' because then you can overlook the absence of the mountain." Skiing in Duluth should be advertised: "Enjoy our brief hill and have a quick ride back to the top."

And, now, in February these tourists are stuck in Duluth because their car wasn't up to near-Siberian conditions. There just has to be a real Duluth, with real people, with Scandinavian heritages, with charming and warming ethnic customs, with landscapes and lakescapes just waiting to be experienced and discovered as the Tourist Bureau suggests. But because Duluth is such an active place in its own right, it's hard to locate what the Tourist Bureau advertises. You have to be persistent if you want to find the *real* Duluth.

The way the Tourist Bureau promotes Duluth as a winter paradise, you'd have to believe Adam and Eve found and peeled the forbidden fruit here at the Head-O-The Lakes. But if you come, bring warm clothing, and lots of money; be prepared to sit out the rain, cold, fog, mosquitoes, blackflies, and armyworms. By all means have enough foresight to bring along a thick book, like Crime & Punishment or *Adventures Through the Lower Colon with Gun & Camera: A Surgeon's First-Hand Experience in Bowel Blockage*. Tourists, be ingenious, canny, and creative; be able to manufacture your own fun if you plan on having any real fun in Duluth.

Nothing gives more pleasure to a Duluthian than sidling up to a stranded tourist and saying "Geez, I bet you didn't check your antifreeze for minus forty below before you left Minneapolis, Edina, or Indiana!" (or wherever the tourist came from, with the exception of Wisconsin; most Duluthians don't tease people from Wisconsin — the "flat-lander, cheese-heads," as they're called by petty detractors — because Duluthians regard them as wealthy, but distant, relatives who somehow survive better on tourism than all of northeastern Minnesota).

Then, of course, the Duluthian, winking at his peers who likewise stop to watch the tourist's demise, adds something like, "Ooohhh boy, it's too bad there aren't any service stations downtown. It's too bad you're at the bottom of the hill. Maaybee, you could have started the car on compression. I guess the closest service station is about two miles away, and you're dressed in such flimsy winter-wear. I hope you got one of those fancy, aHH-toe-MOW-beel credit cards that let's you get a jumpstart or towing services. I heard tell, it sometimes takes two days to unfreeze a car at this temperature."

Duluthians can give world-class, inspirational advice when it comes to aiding tourists in cold weather. But that's not all. For life in Duluth to have real meaning, Duluthians willingly share their experience and folk wisdom, giving it to tourists whenever they can be found. Giving advice is one thing Duluthians are extremely conscientious about. It's doubtful that many tourists have made it through Duluth without getting some free advice at a gas station, a motel, or even from restaurant waiters, the latter being able to give up-to-date mercury counts in Lake Superior fish catches and fog arrival and departure reports.

Most advice Duluthians offer is the regional conventional kind. It is historic, such as "You should have been here last week. Why, the sun was so hot, you could see the ice melting in the lake right down on the beach at Park Point."

Or, Duluth tourist advice prompts sure hysteria. "Ohhh, you're going to drive up there?! Well, if I was you, I'd get some heavy-duty bug spray and be certain to carry a couple of bags of sand in your trunk. I hear tell those armyworms are so dense that cars slide right off the road. Why, last week, my cousin, Elaine, had to walk in front of the car spreading sand, while her husband, Frank, drove. To hear her tell it, those armyworms were so thick on the road she could hardly keep from slipping. I mean ... are you sure you really want to see Chester Park?" (A park found more or less smack in the middle of town.)

Aside from the counsel on dealing with the unseasonable weather year-round, liberal Duluth advice is one of the reasons the homeless don't stick around long; they complain that they get free advice, at great personal loss, but nothing permanent. Well, this is the real Duluth spirit, since nothing is permanent; the more things change, the more they really do change for the worse, as Duluthians espouse in their downhill philosophy. What they don't tell you, of course, is that things are going mostly downhill for everybody else, but not entirely for them, personally, which can make a person wonder about things.

Fortunately, though, once the *really cold* weather hits Duluth and stays around long enough to restore an appropriate degree of authentic fatalism and dourness, Duluthians start really wondering

Just Keep Going North..

about things. A Duluthian wondering is a potent force, almost as awesome as a Calvinist rising from bended knees after prayer.

What Duluthians wonder about, however, takes a peculiar bent, like making forecasts, guessing about things, and trying to make predictions. A "wondering Duluthian" logically winds up with a sense of the important; wondering, for Duluthians, sorts out the many trivial thoughts from the critical few. These critical few thoughts are what sustain Duluthians across the seasons, well into their thirties and beyond. Duluthians keep these thoughts under wraps most of the time, although some such thought gems pop out as questions, show up in city ordinances, and even appear in the "Letters to the Editor."

Since some of these deep thoughts do surface periodically (such as the need for mental flossing or counting family members), they almost inevitably lead to predictions. Predictions, such as the lack of success of the legislative team down-state, generally come true; there never is enough money available for the Arrowhead Region.

These wonderings occupy the thoughts of Duluthians and they build on them. They devise really important ideas, like when will the seagulls return to the sanitary landfill north of town (the one that used to be called the city dump), and how many seagulls will make it through the winter to arrive in the spring out there or down at the harbor? You can be sure this is a hot topic with the noontime crowd down at Fitgers. There's even a seagull contest at the Happy Fisherfolk Restaurant.

The wondering doesn't stop there. Duluthians are captivated by wondering when the first ship will pass through the ship canal; will it be a laker or a saltie? Or, when will the last clothing store on Superior Street shut down and move to the mall? Duluthians don't want to bet on this sort of thing because it's going to happen sooner or later. Like many things in Duluth, it's just a matter of time — most people won't know the difference.

None of these questions and predictions are earthshaking and may even seem a bit parochial, but then you have to make do with what you've got. People stopped guessing about when any kind of industry might return to Duluth, because that's too complex. Duluthians tend to go more for yes or no, today or tomorrow, black or white, kinds of questions. After all, you need to occupy your mind

Just Keep Going North..

with something if you live in Duluth. The unimaginable alternatives would be nothing short of fantasy stuff used to write short stories. You sure can't talk about international finance, computer viruses, or even pasta futures with Duluthians. Bring up one of these topics and Duluthians will quietly suffer a melt-down. They mentally go on strike if something beyond U.M.-D. hockey, the weather, or bus service is raised in conversation, or posed as a question. So, it stands to reason that water pipes can make the headlines in Duluth. Do you doubt it? Read on.

Chapter twelve

Most People Won't Even Know The Difference

Well, they changed the city water service in certain parts of town. It's pretty complicated, so that means it likely involved the City Water & Gas, the City Engineering, and the Public Works departments; that combination of players is bound to make things more complex than most people can handle whether they live in Duluth, Superior, or even Tacoma. It goes without saying that had the City Legal Department been added to the other ingredients, the story might have been covered by down-state television. Those Twin City news people are always eager to make Duluth look bad, but they missed their chance this time.

As the story has it, events almost reached a point of concern greater than most Duluthians are willing to bear, since everything seemed to be going downhill faster than usual.

It all started out back in December, when the temperature dropped to its normal range of zero, day and night. About that time a number of East Hillside residents started to complain that their water pressure was too low. Of course, nobody in the City Water & Gas Department paid much, if any, attention since the temperature wasn't cold enough to cause more than normal problems, which usually means about ten times worse than customary by Twin City standards.

Since those East Hillsiders are conspicuous complainers, no one in city operations took them seriously. Yet, City Water & Gas sent a person out to check the matter over. He spent most of the afternoon over at his brother's place on East 10th Street. Since there was obviously nothing else to do or say, nothing much was done except to prepare a three-page report based on solid impressions and reasonably subjective "walk-about" data, which is good enough for phase A-1.0 type problems in Duluth.

But two weeks before Christmas, things did get a little out of hand; if you want to know how things get rolling downhill in Duluth, you'd better pay attention from here on out.

It all started when Maxine Sturm went to lunch with Julie Maki. Now, you have to understand that Maxine's been with City

Just Keep Going North..

Water & Gas for close to thirty years, that she's a past Matron in the Eastern Star, past president of the Downtown Business Women's League, and her husband retired from the Burlington last March. Then there's Julie Maki. She's from the big downtown newspaper, some kind of an editor, and she is also a big factor, way up, in the ranks of Duluth Eastern Star. Maxine doesn't bowl anymore because of her back injury, but Julie still belongs to a Highland League.

Anyway, Julie and Maxine have been having lunch together for some fifteen years, on Mondays, usually at the Chinese Platter, because they like those melted Velveeta cheese Monte Cristo sandwiches on the menu.

Now, these types of Duluthians are not prone to gossip. But to ensure utter privacy Maxine cupped her hand and whispered to Julie — like it was some Eastern Star secret — that the whole problem about water pressure on the East Hillside was just a lot of baloney or some words to that effect. (Eastern Star people don't tend to use very strong language, and, in fact, most Duluthians don't use a whole lot of sentences at one time, much less even think in paragraphs.) It didn't take much for Julie to get the picture. And, since she lives up there on the East Hillside, she understood what Maxine's few whispered words meant right away.

Maxine had said something like pipeline freeze-ups. And, that was all that was said, because there were other matters these two Duluthians had to discuss, and it would be impolite, even pointless, to ask what they were; some things simply are better left unwritten, especially if one is married to a retired railroad employee and another's lover suffers from periodic impotence. But the less said the better in order to get to the really important story.

By 2:30 that afternoon Julie was back at the *NooStribune*. She had made a few phone calls and was going over some clippings when she off-handedly mentioned this idea of the pipeline freeze-ups to the sports editor, Verne ("Big Schuss") Edelstrom, but never mentioning the source, naturally.

Yet, the next day on page two, there it was in the *NooStribune* for all of Duluth to read, with coffee and powdered doughnut holes.

Just Keep Going North..

WATER & GAS DEPT. CLAIMS PIPE FREEZE-UPS: HILLSIDE PROBLEM.

According to a recent report obtained from the Duluth Water & Gas Department, household pipeline freeze-ups are the major cause of East Hillside concerns. Complaints of many East Hillside residents that water pressure is the major factor are unfounded. The report blames East Hillside residents for failing to take adequate in-house protection against winter weather. As DW & G inspector, Eric Lindahl, reported: *"The residents have not done enough to protect their own in-house water service lines, with freezing now the natural result. It's unfortunate these residents have the problem, and DW & G is doing what it can to survey the extent of household concern."* The report concluded that water pressure was normal for these months.

So, maybe the problem wasn't just low water pressure; maybe the problem was pipeline freeze-ups. The article went on to say that not enough of those East Hillsiders had taken advantage of the city-sponsored home insulation program, for a modest charge somewhere between $300 and $800. So it was just common sense that East Hillsiders should have taken appropriate action sooner, when they could have prevented the problem.

Well, in Duluth, problem-solving works best if blame and guilt can be assigned and spread pretty thick, if you can be sure that those deemed guilty won't fight back. But, those East Hillsiders have got real gumption. They hadn't heard about any report before now, they hadn't been contacted, and they didn't believe what the *Noo-Stribune* had to say, which was both constructively radical and destructively reactionary in the extreme for East Hillsiders.

When this report hit the East Hillside, some Hillsiders got pretty mad. It takes a great deal of pressure to get Duluthians agitated, much less even mad or willing to talk about a problem. But this did it! It got those East Hillsiders boiling. Imagine, somebody telling them they should have insulated their pipes, somebody pointing a finger of homeowner neglect at them. Imagine, after they had already paid top-dollar to get their windows and doors insulated, even extra insulation in the attic. In Duluth, this kind of advice is like telling people how many children they should have or what kind of car to buy. Those East Hillsiders, once they get riled up, they won't let go of anything.

Just Keep Going North..

To the East Hillsiders, this newspaper article was like a brakeman's red flag waved in desperation; it meant they were going to dig in their heels and get to the bottom of this. They weren't going to be sidetracked by a report from the City Water & Gas Department when they knew better.

Inspired by their previous experience in dealing with city hall, they organized and attended the City Council meeting on Tuesday night, bringing with them half- and three-quarters-filled plastic milk containers, to illustrate just how much water came out of the tap in a three-minute period. It was their contention that low water pressure was the problem, not pipeline freeze-ups.

Naturally, the City Council members were amazed, not only because this was the first they had actually heard about some water problem, but also at the ingenuity of these East Hillsiders.

The council members sat gingerly on the edges of their oak chairs, thus acknowledging their concern, but incapacity, to deal with citizen needs and interests. The legs of the council members were twisted around their chairs and their feet braced on the carpeted council floor as they suffered through the testimony of these East Hillsiders. But, reminded of their roles as elected officials by the TV crew and production director, they snapped back to business after some twenty minutes of testimony.

Two council members asked the residents repeatedly how they had conducted this research. How had they hit upon this idea? Did they get help from those university people over at U.M.-D., or did the County Extension Service put them up to this?

There was even some shouting, which is quite rare in Duluth, especially in the City Council Chambers, except between the Mayor and the City Council members. One might hear screaming in Duluth when a tourist steps into Lake Superior in July, but otherwise shouting is largely unheard of.

Finally, Carl Bjornquist, one of the councilors-at-large, interrupted the proceedings with a motion, the motion being a folding and re-folding of his hands. You may think that Carl is sleeping up there behind the council table, but he's more of a "closed-lid" listener.

Carl leaned his 270 pounds forward, tugged at his starched collar, and in his deepest red-faced voice, said, "We can't have people in Duluth getting just a half or even a three-quarter's bottle of water.

Just Keep Going North..

People in Duluth deserve a full bottle of water and that's what we're going to give 'em."

That remark and the ensuing request for deeper study of the problem drew applause from all the East Hillside residents in the council chamber; even four of the seven council members applauded. It wasn't clear or why or what they were applauding. They mostly take their cues now from the TV crew telecasting Council proceedings. It turns out that votes on some twenty-eight motions were directed by the TV producer, much to the surprise of the Council members, but not at all surprising to Duluth audiences.

On the following day, you can be sure the City Engineering and Public Works departments got a priority memo from the mayor's office. By noon, Public Works had started removing the lids to access water mains along the streets, from 4th Street to the Skyline Drive, between 6th Avenue and 15th Avenue East, to inspect the water mains and to check for pressure defects.

Of course, in the winter it's a bit easier to deal with water mains and the like than in the summer when it's raining; these city workers really know how to deal with the permafrost conditions. So, in less than two days — by December 16 — it was clear there was a problem, and it wasn't those pipes freezing in the resident's homes.

In addition to blocking off some forty-two intersections, which caused traffic tie-ups in the alleys, it was clear there was a pressure problem and it wasn't limited to water alone. There was pressure on the City Engineering and Public Works departments to find and name that problem, since in Duluth, you don't have a problem until someone in authority names it.

By late Friday afternoon, with the Mayor on one end of the telephone line, the City Engineering Department named the problem. It was called "excessive independent water flow demand." That sounded pretty good! It was just technical enough to sound like no other current problem in Duluth, which was fitting and proper. Secondly, it was obvious enough to suggest an immediate solution, which appeared in the Sunday *NooStribune*. In naming a problem in Duluth, you must also imply the solution, and City Engineering had the solution.

Since water service in Duluth is mostly continuous, it would be a simple matter to shift to batch-servicing, which, when it was explained to people, seemed to make sense. It meant people could get a full bottle of water more or less, which was after all what would satisfy both the customers and the City Council members.

By Tuesday of the next week, notices had been mailed to all East Hillside residents, inviting them to attend a neighborhood meeting on either December 24 or December 3l, in the basement of the 1st Spiritualist Church, located on the corner of 13th Avenue East and 9th Street, scheduled for 7:00 a.m both days.

The public notice indicated that the Water & Gas Department chief would be there, along with City Engineering staff, to present and defend their proposal. This proposal was simplicity itself.

Stressing the importance of sharing and caring this holiday season, of being a good citizen and the like, City Engineering proposed that on *odd* hours of the day, people living on the *avenues* would get full water pressure, while people living on the *streets* would get full water pressure on the *even* hours of the day, twenty-four hours a day. It seems it was just a matter of installing some shunts and a timer valve in the water mains.

Admittedly, the solution to the problem had a certain amount of face validity, since it paralleled the rules and regulations for winter parking, odd side and even side. Most residents took it for granted that this was an acceptable and logical extension of odd-even thinking. After all, it was good to know that odd and even were something you could count on. A good principle should be extended and enhanced; it should be used universally rather than dreaming up some untried idea.

And, in Duluth, odd and even makes a lot of sense. One should see how really odd people drive and park in Duluth; one should experience how hard Duluth legislators try to even the score against those oddball down-state opponents; and one has to experience on a day-to-day basis how uneven the odds are for human survival in Duluth for the oddest reasons. Odd-even values are part of the Duluth mind-set and they seem to work.

The residents at the meetings expressed their relief in knowing that their concerns had been dealt with by city hall. At least some did.

The fact that several U.M.-D. faculty members, also East Hillside residents, thought the idea was absurd, even asinine, made no difference. They were in the minority. The majority of people attending the meeting held views akin to Ethel Hammerstrom's, who

Just Keep Going North..

had never before been in the Spiritualist Church. She nudged her husband and whispered so the spirits wouldn't hear. "Isn't that just like those university people? They're always trying to object to everything when we know what it's really like living in Duluth. Imagine those people trying to come in here and tell those Water & Gas people how to run their business. It's shameless."

    Pulling her deep blue fabric coat more tightly around her body and clutching her purse, Ethel Hammerstrom sat there enthralled as these city officials continued to spar with the newcomers. Like other old-timers who attended such public meetings, she knew she just wanted water in her home. The thought of how much and when was suddenly less important than wondering whether there was a bathroom in this church ... and would it be safe to use it alone. This was going to be better than World Federation Wrestling, she thought to herself, as she suppressed other needs less salient than just listening to a good argument, complete with a lot of technical words. Duluthians like the sounds of new technical words: it adds to their wonderment fund.

    One East Hillside resident, Paul Hinton, PhD, from U.M.-D.'s Speech & Communications Arts Department, called the proposal "retrograde," adding, "Imagine, just imagine, any other city this size providing water this way! Batch-servicing? You have to be kidding," he said.

    "You bet it's retrograde," replied the City Engineering official, "but then most people won't know the difference. We factored in the angle of the hills and then down-graded the entire problem. We differentiated the vertical and horizontal incline of the water gradient, mainline volume, and subtracted the age of the pumping equipment. You didn't think we'd overlook those simple factors, did you?"

    Convinced by the quiet admiration he inspired, the City Engineer even went so far as to suggest that he didn't think Dr. Hinton had a degree in engineering and was thereby playing horseshoes in a situation that called for real hardball thinking. There were no other objections. It was an open and shut case, black and white, just the way Duluthians like things.

    Well, that City Engineer's performance was talked about downtown as if it were a real knockdown, drag-out verbal duel. A number of people expressed regret at having missed the public

Just Keep Going North..

hearings, because the occasions for any public debate — especially between real professionals — are so rare in Duluth.

To the East Hillsiders, the solution was secondary to the method for having arrived at such an elegantly serviceable idea. The importance of having an odd and even life-organizing principle was reaffirmed. After all, if you have to have rules in life, have good ones and then stick to them. That's crucial to overall well-being in Duluth, and newcomers and tourists alike have to recognize that simple fact of life.

So, as it stands, a large number of the East Hillside residents will have their water batch-serviced starting this week. That news almost made it to the Twin Cities.

Actually, the change to the batched water service took a little longer than planned — about six weeks longer — what with the surprise snowstorm, the need to flood the ice-skating rinks, the winter vacation schedules of the Public Works employees, and the cold weather.

Of course, if any resident insists upon regular, continuous water service, well, that's available at an additional cost of eight cents a cubic foot, plus a pressure reducer and equalizer valve installed on the premises for an added annual cost of $112.76, plus city tax.

One of the neighbors said he'd heard there was a motion before the City Council to create alternating odd-even address numbers for streets and avenues if this new water service system works out. But he thought that ordinance wouldn't pass, because it goes without saying in Duluth: most people won't even know the difference.

Chapter thirteen

It's The Same Every Fall

The sameness of the past week in Duluth came close to breaking the all-time record set back in 1947. The past week was almost a triumph in terms of recorded dullness and uneventfulness. If the clouds had formed a deeper gray blanket, and if the fog and drizzle had been more constant, there's no doubt a new record would have been set. This sort of everydayness was average for mid-autumn, as it is generally for Duluth. The sun popped out Wednesday, at about 4:00 p.m., just long enough to lift some of the fog from around the downtown area, after which the gray sameness returned with full vigor. It was probably that brief glimmer of sunshine that prevented the new record from being set. Lakeside residents — out there on the eastern stretch along the lake — probably haven't seen the sun since last week. But not surprisingly, all one has to do is drive over the Duluth hills toward the Miller Mall, toward Pike Lake, or even Cloquet, to experience a bright and sunny sky with just the right number of cottony clouds.

To believers, this is about all the evidence needed to prove that climate, science, and politics are in their right and proper place. It's reassuring for Duluthians to know that this "lesser trinity" united to plan it that way, lest Duluthians feel they were receiving undue, even premature, punishment for unnamed and undisclosed sins. Duluthians know they chose to live where they do; it's only the consequences thereof that matter at all to anybody. And, there hangs the story.

Yep, it's September. It's the time of year to get mentally prepared for what's ahead, now that those tourists have gone back to wherever they came from and crossed Duluth off their list of exciting places. It's during these kinds of weeks that a whole bunch of Duluthians start airing out their plaid mackinaws and winter coats, dusting off those matching plaid bib caps, and examining their Sorel boots for wear and tear. The dry-cleaning establishments do a pretty fair business at this time of year, and even the shoe-repair shops get busy, what with putting black patches on those four-buckle galoshes and tire patches on the Sorels where the snow-blowers

Just Keep Going North..

nicked them. So, it's time to get down to serious business and think about survival from a couple of different angles.

It just takes a few frosted mornings to turn Duluthians into a different lot. They're out in the garden with boxes picking the last of the tomatoes and the few remaining apples, washing storm windows, and re-arranging snow shovels and tools in their garages, and doing lots of house inspection.

Like "pluffing," house inspection is a Head-O-The-Lakes sport; it provides a bit of fun before winter. Scoring is easy. A householder simply walks around the outside of the house and points at various defects, such as a plug of missing putty, a cracked window, or a loose shingle. Extra points are earned if a neighbor or relative gets conned into the game of pointing out the problems that must be taken care of soon. Mostly, the game is played solo, by just walking around the house, pointing at a problem and mumbling something like, "Boy, I gotta' take care of that before winter gets here," or "Geez, that's real bad. How'd that happen? Gotta' take care of that before the snow flies!"

Duluthians are pretty good at pointing out problems. The kids learn it at an early age, as they help drag a stepladder from window to window, listening to a parent mutter and complain about how the paint is loose on the shutters or how the aluminum siding color is fading. By the time these youngsters are in high school, they've mastered the art of problem detection. Typical remarks include: "Hey, Dad, did you know the gas is on empty?" or "Mom, did you know there's no pizza in the freezer?"

It's a wonder more Duluthians aren't hired to deal with the concerns of the state and federal government, given their abilities to point out our problems. But, maybe being able to point out a loose piece of siding or a cracked storm window frame isn't exactly the full house of credentials needed to deal with mega-loans to private industry, revenue shortfalls, or property tax formulas. Then again, who knows? Who really knows?

Being able to point out a problem, especially somebody else's problem — a problem they didn't even know existed — is clearly a local talent. Maybe it's a by-product of life up here in the North Country, a kind of nature-nurture driven mannerism. The neighbors think it's inborn, maybe even a locally induced survival trait, or a mutation that gives Duluthians a slight edge over everyday life. I guess, if you got right down to it, if a scientist put some Duluth genes under a microscope, they would only show what everybody already knows: some of that chromosome material ain't exactly hooked up the way it's supposed to be. I'd guess that scientist would see those chromosomes arranged quite nicely for subsistence living, all twenty-two pairs, plus the X and Y, in the shape of a helical snowflake.

(It seems that way back in the 1970s one of those down-state scientists did a study that showed there was a real biological type emerging in Duluth, an offshoot of the Minnesota species. That scientist went on to claim that isolation, over-involvement with hockey, and other forms of cultural inbreeding might be the cause, but she was pretty vague about what that new species might resemble. Hells bells, you can't always expect a scientist to put pictures to words, much less ever go down to Shorty's Bar, hit the Kosy Korner on a Saturday night, or meet everybody in town. Of course, some of neighbors wondered if that scientist might have confused real Duluthians with tourists, especially those from the Twin Cities. It could happen, and so another intriguing theory was tossed briefly onto the trash heap of mid-range science. The neighbors, however, think the idea has some merit. They think scientists will probably discover the socio-genetic basis for *Homo duluthiensis northlandii* in a few years, if they can sort out the jetsam from the flotsam of environmentally altered genes. It will probably show that this new, emerging human species has a few more liver spots than freckles, thicker skin from where the windchill index attacks and leaves its characteristic worry lines, a lot of hair — thick hair that grows out at odd angles from under a permanently worn baseball cap — and a curiously whimsical smile that borders on sarcasm. For any younger bio-social scientists, it's well worth coming to Duluth in search of the Duluth/Northland bio-type. Documenting this type could mean instant fame in scientific circles or squares, depending on which journal publishes the article.)

Anyway, it's fall and what's supposed to happen is under way. It's time to start covering the roses, check those storm windows and do a bit of putty work on them, and otherwise button down the hatches, because snow can come anytime now. The first few snowflakes that are often sent in September act like a whip to remind Duluthians to get going, to take action, and to prepare for what's ahead.

Just Keep Going North..

Chapter fourteen

Life's Little Stumbling Blocks

U.M.-D. is something like a miniature "Big U," and includes a scrappy, but bantam-sized faculty, bite-sized intellectual life, and a scaled-down curriculum, where the latter is subject to re-organization and culling with each new administrator. Everything at U.M.-D. is tentative or probational, subject to down-state, Big U approval, which fits right in with the overall tactics in higher and lower education on the Duluth scene. So, if anything looks like it might succeed at U.M.-D., you can be sure the Big U types have their monkeywrenches ready to fix that problem. Consequently, not much succeeds on its own two feet at U.M.-D., except a tenacious survival mentality and an "under construction" regional mission.

(Nobody seems to know how U.M.-D. gets funded, much less how dollars are spent over there, because it's all a huge secret kept down-state, encrypted in mysterious accounting language. Some local legislators reported that the Academic & Financial Vice Presidents from the Big U sit down with the Chancellor and the Provost from U.M.-D. and play a game called, "You & Me Gotta' Problem," which includes dice, a four-color board very nicely done up, a whip, and such language as, "I get twelve for me and here's one for you, and so I get an extra turn; I get mine now, but you get yours later; and, I get to go to the legislature, you get to go nowhere. We get to do research and you get to do studies," and so forth. I don't know what the whip is for, but maybe it has something to do with setting the pace of the game.)

Well, it so happened one day that the Duluth media broadcast a mid-morning report about a university uproar, the worst demonstration since the Vietnam era. It should be known that such news just riles up Duluthians no end; they think they have to respond to it by writing "Letters to the Editor." And, so it happened that this news reached Duluth through the deviltry of the media, who knew full well what the impacts would likely be upon Duluthians.

It all began over at the Big U, when the news was leaked (on purpose by an administrator in the academic vice president's office, assigned such duties based on extensive personality dysfunction and a $85,000 salary) that financial problems facing the university would mean cutbacks, department mergers, and a salary freezes. Yep, the university was told to dig into its "hidden resource accounts" and come up with $35 million. It defies imagination why the legislature felt the university system would suffer at all from this meager loss. The university system can raise $35 million simply by looking under its academic gown, by a flick of its collegial wrist, without even eliminating unnecessary services or raising tuition. But it was the merger idea that frightened the university faculty the most, because turf wars are the real politics of academic life.

As every Minnesotan knows, such mergers, say, of foreign language departments, even economics and business, are as incompatible as trying to blend the Heisenberg principle with Murphy's Law and then trying to justify that action by multiplying it all by 1929 gas prices. It simply is academically and organizationally impossible to merge faculty whose hearts are set on owning their own special piece of turf without expecting furor and internecine warfare conducted with no strategy except control of the copying machine and travel funds to professional meetings.

That's how some things work in the academic world, not well, but at least as transparently self-serving as possible. The true spirit of academic freedom and professionalism is the right to be dead wrong rather than to be wrongfully disabused of any academic pretensions. Pretensions, like foibles, take a long time to develop their leafy arrogance and deep-rooted ambitions. Humility does not have much cash value when it comes to academic pretensions or high-powered university political games.

But now things had gotten out of hand. Some shrewd outsider-type administrators had snuck into pen-holder positions of power and had scribbled and sent the message to departments helter-skelter: You gotta' merge and do it fast. These administrators had found the weak point. Merger ... aggregating protagonists, as one administrator gleefully termed it ... cost reductions ... even requiring that senior faculty teach!

As the news spread across throughout the university system, it was apparent that trouble was brewing and it was brewing faster than egg-coffee over at the Sons of Norway Lodge 219 annual winter meeting. "Hold to the status quo" was the main position held by faculty who whispered the correct words and phrases to the protestors. The noise and commotion caused lectures and learning to be

Just Keep Going North..

halted in mid-epigram as the battlecries of volunteer-protestors signaled their efforts to control both turf and academic policy.

Meanwhile back in Duluth, a startling message came across the airwaves, one carefully chosen to heighten Duluthians' confusion.

"We have a report from several U of M campuses that students and faculty are engaging in what appears to be the major protest demonstration of the season," broke in the Duluth disc jockey and newscaster. "It seems U of M students and faculty across the state have taken over several buildings in a protest over forced mergers and possible tuition hikes. It appears university departments are being asked to teach, that's right, to teach students, and the report says that this has angered faculty, who have taken to the streets in protest.

"The report adds that the faculty are being asked to undertake relevant research, research that might have some practical value, possibly to Minnesota or elsewhere, and to bring in outside funding to support their research efforts themselves. This early report indicates the professors want to preserve their right to do independent, self-serving research and consulting, and are seeking guarantees to that effect. Recent funding cutbacks have meant few ten percent salary increases. This has angered the faculty, a few of whom thought the game plan was 'Pretend to be Pursuing Excellence,' while the real game under way is 'If You Have A Department, It Only Costs a Bit More to Go First Class.'"

"The information is very sketchy at this time. Administrators are preparing for a long siege in their panelled offices. We will keep you posted as developments come into this station. Now, let's get back to that good ol' country western stuff."

This muddled news hit the U. M.-D. campus like lightening on a clear humid day in the B.W.C.A., and then spread like wildfire. Having experienced re-organization so often, the fear of one more effort to re-juggle departments, to teach and do research, plus outreach, hit that campus on its blind-side. It bred panic among some faculty, aided by the coffee-break network of the clerical support staff.

The news report was the final proof needed to convince some faculty that things could only improve under such a monumental merger idea, while other faculty vehemently opposed the concept. It

Just Keep Going North..

further divided faculty into the "whiners and complainers," into passive-aggressives, dominant orthodox and heterodox dogmatic, and compliant subordinate types (as several social psychologists later testified at the academic hearings for dismissal and tenure-removal).

Things quickly got out of hand over at U.M.-D., as they had across the university system. Several U.M.-D. administrators, including the Chancellor-in-Residence, straightaway suffered anxiety attacks on hearing this news, thereby prompting their self-removal from the scene of further possible dispute. The battle, if it was going to be fought at U.M.-D., would have to be handled by the assistants to the associate vice-presidents, as best they could.

With fear as their motive, those U.M.-D. faculty were no slouches in responding to things going on across the university system. They used seasoned intellectual combat techniques, since there were a number of department vultures waiting to pounce on any weaker department that wandered too far away from its intellectual origins.

For starters, the Athletic Department sent over the football team to guard Darland and Bohannon Hall, which the coaches thought was a good idea in general since it would allow them to practice certain social skills in teaming and crowd control. And it was a good idea until the Woman's Study faculty and its 110 strong majors (who had their eye on the History, Sociology, and Special Education departments) began a verbal assault on those behemoths, calling them sexist, and chauvinists, and using words that made those football players blush. The clincher came when the women's basketball team, the Lady Bull-Dog hoopsters, broke right through the line and sent those football players scampering back to the Sports & Health Center, with words under their breath that don't need comment at this point, but required no translation down at the Reefy Bar.

Unfortunately, the U.M.-D. library was left unguarded, and someone crept in surreptitiously and removed both books. The loss went unnoticed for more than six hours. The Computer Engineering Department unleased a whole batch of new computer viruses, willy-nilly, into the electronic mail networks. Imagine her surprise when Greta Darby, the secretary over in the Student Loan Office, was hit with the message: "HI THERE. Your system is stoned. Your memory will begin to fail in six nanoseconds and will be inoperative for the next ten days."

The Social Work unit assembled as a group dynamics exercise to rightly reference itself, and then proceeded to parade in full academic regalia through the hallways and campus streets. They were led by their director, who held the unit's certificate of accreditation aloft. Using New Age rhythms, the group chanted in unison sotto voce, "WE TOO Are ccredited/Accredited are WE, TOO." This socio-drama prompted some students to fall to their knees as the relic of accreditation — emblazoned with a shiny gold seal and illegible signatures — passed by. The candle-bearers and incense added a nice touch.

Prompted by the news from down-state, the intellectual divisions of U.M.-D. did not follow conventional lines, such as soft- or hard-headed science, relevant or irrelevant. Rather, it all boiled down to which faculty had earned a "go-by" name and which had not. It didn't matter who had written the most about Great Lakes shipwrecks, Lake County fauna and flora, or which instructors were most fearsome. It mattered more that some faculty had gotten a really good go-by name from students, like Kami I & II for the two economists who lecture largely facing the blackboard with macro- and micro-intoned, formula-inspired, voices. The senior chemistry professor was known as Garf and the plant manager was Twinx; Eeekie was the Food Service director's go-by name, and there were many others who have just as good go-by names. And, as you know, having a go-by name means being part of the Duluth crowd. People with go-by names stick together.

As reported on the evening TV, it seems some of the U.M.-D. faculty stooped to near bottom-line ethics in their efforts to stave off further budget cuts and mergers. The group with go-by names (that must remain nameless) hit on a plan for just such an eventuality, not a great plan as plans go, but striking in its boldness. Racing to the hidden intellectual weapon storage area, maintained just for such occasions, these faculty members quickly removed predetermined journal articles authored by their mediocre opposition, the name-less ones, who had pretensions beyond their ability to teach, do research, and provide outreach. That faculty force then began reading — outloud — in front of the faculty member's door, those articles and research reports the name-less ones had written. Imagine the heart-pounding embarrassment and defensive feelings evoked when a

Just Keep Going North..

stranger reads your favorite article aloud, right outside your office door and in several student lounge areas.

Some of the most ridiculed papers included one of the associate vice president's papers, "Halloween Tricks or Treats Comparatives: North Carolina versus Southern Idaho — Frequency of Hershey Bar Distribution versus Mars Bars in Educationally & Economically Enriched Neighborhoods," and Professor Maxwell-Smything's masterpiece, "Theoretic Polymorphic Non-Crystallization Distributions & Molecular Collapse of Urethane when Theoretically Embedded, Chelated and Otherwise Subjected to Mind-Only Tests Beyond Its Intended Structural Limits & Use."

As the protest reached its peak on the Main U and its nadir at the Zenith City of the North, on the U. M.-D. campus, things got sorted out rather fast, as learning tends to do when knowledge is no longer a stumbling block. The consensus was quickly reached that it might be necessary to ask non-Minnesotan faculty and administrators to hang their academic garb and pretensions in the closet, and to get to work drafting and living up to real position descriptions, with quality accountabilities built-in, and maybe even after honest-to-goodness work analysis. Persons who would scarcely be expected to identify with Minnesota could be taught some fundamentals of what Minnesota expects from its academics. And scholars who felt they were gracing Minnesota by their presence might find it more sensible, if not more stimulating, to find a perch elsewhere.

Naturally, these events had to end sooner or later. They did when the President of the Big U, bowing to pressure from the collection of professional associations and quasi-consulting firms housed throughout the university at taxpayer expense — postured as teaching, research, and outreach departments — delayed the decisions on cutbacks and mergers. Departments were safe for awhile. The whole situation needed further study, perhaps well into his successor's term of office. There would be no more talk about vague needs to restore quality standards and fiscal integrity under operating necessity on any campus of this university, at least not for some time. Nope, there wasn't going to be a week available for such issues for a long time, if ever.

"When one bull charges, you gotta' chance; when a whole herd of bulls get angry and attacks, it's time to get outta' that

Just Keep Going North..

pasture," is how the President of the Big U related this experience to a wide-eyed Board of Regents, as he once more tried to submit his resignation.

But, maybe, just maybe, something good came out of all this turmoil. In their enthusiasm to challenge with ideas, those protestors at U.M.-D. had pasted thirty to forty opened and unopened Minnesota lottery tickets on the door of the Addiction Studies Center. The program director scornfully tore those tickets down, but not before checking each one. It turned out that one of the protestors (more likely than not a Green) was willing to forego cashing in a bona-fide lottery ticket for $250,000. And, that's how the word got out. The neighbors have been wondering what the Director of the Addiction Studies Center did with that ticket.

If the Addiction Center is strapped for money and no new funds were forthcoming from university or other sources to help explain why people drink, swear, gamble, or have other addictive behaviors, like fishing or penny-ante poker, what would that director do with such conceivably morally tainted lottery money? After all, money obtained through the gambling habits of the weak-willed and gullible surely couldn't be used to support an Addiction Studies Center ... or could it?

Most of the neighbors want to know if knowledge really is the stumbling block to life-long fulfillment that it's made out to be — like learning what happened to that lottery ticket good for something like $250,000. Was that ticket cashed in or not and by whom?

Well, you won't get that information in this story. You see, knowledge really is a stumbling block that fascinates open and closed minds. You almost got too close to knowing something you shouldn't even be thinking about at all. Like you shouldn't be thinking about whether U.M.-D. needs an Addiction Study Center, much less whether anybody but the professional staff will ever benefit from finding out what causes addictive fishing behavior or why people who lose five dollars by their self-indulgence in penny-ante poker will go right on playing that game next Saturday night. Don't think about it!

And, you shouldn't be thinking about whether that $250,000 went into the personal account of the Addiction Study Center director, or even what happened to that money. That's the real Duluth spirit — learning what not to think about and what that means. At

99

Just Keep Going North..

least that's what the neighbors conclude. It doesn't mean that lottery ticket has been forgotten, not at all. It just means that the real addiction is knowledge, and you gotta' give that up if you're going to survive in Duluth. After all, foibles are so much more enjoyable than knowledge. And it's foibles that will earn you a good go-by name, not knowledge.

Just Keep Going North..

Chapter fifteen

What's There To Say

This last week in June will likely go down in Duluth history, as it rightly should, for a most memorable event, which was signaled immediately by the downtown paper, the NooStribune. Sometimes you have to force yourself to read beyond the headlines, even to page two of the local bird-cage liner and fish wrap, which is exactly where this great event was signaled. It read: "Finn to Speak." Need I elaborate, except for those readers who might want some inkling as to what this could possibly mean?

To any reading Duluthians, it meant the NooStribune had probably made a mistake; the paper really meant "McFinn to Speak," or "Sam Fine to Speak," or even "The Divine to Speak." Breathlessly, readers waited until the next day, presuming, as often happens, that a "Correction in Copy" would appear. You can be sure that this announcement in the premier Northland print media, as it stood, prompted more than casual comment during coffee breaks city-wide; it evoked responses ranging from quiet disbelief to outright amazement, as the neighbors relate the story.

Nothing showed up the next day to alter the story as originally printed, nor the day after, or even five days after that announcement. By then the certainty of the newspaper's version hit Duluthians. "Finn to Speak" at public gathering even started to interfere with their conscious states. Such an event could have earthshaking implications.

For many Duluthians this idea was no less significant than Houdini's prophecy that he would make contact from the "other side," while others felt it had the awesome potential of a papal encyclical on space visitors, or even held some fundamental clue about the prospects for setting a date and time for the Second Coming.

How would this Finn do it, and where? Would there be soft melodious chimes or celestial background music? What would this Finn have to say? Would it be a heavenly mandate, an Eleventh or Twelfth Commandment? And, *why* would this Finn want to speak?

Just Keep Going North..

These thoughts raced through the minds of Duluthians, like bonus points being scored on an out-of-kilter pinball machine.

Everybody in Duluth knows Finns are the hardest working, thriftiest, down-to-earth people in the Northland, not to mention being practical and ingenious. Best of all, Finns smile and laugh a lot, which tends to set them apart from most other Duluthians. They have an inexhaustible sense of humor even after a few drinks, which is more than can be said for those belligerent types out at the Vulcan Bar in Gary/New Duluth. There's something in the makeup of Finnish people, even in the fourth generation immigrant stock, that's kept them even-keeled and laughing in the face of adversity. But, never purposely anger a Finn or you might find yourself in the "twilight zone" of life, dead and buried, faster than you could say Saantanapetikka.

It's OK, for example, if a Finn saddles up to you after a few boilermakers, and asks, in a low voice, "Can you speak Finnish a little bit these days?" There's only one right answer: "No, not today, but yesterday I did." This joker will then ask you, "So, you don't even understand Finnish, right?" The correct answer again is "No, but I'm thinking about learnin' it." Then you're going to hear, "Vymyalotta, you're dumber than a Finn!" It's that sort of self-deprecating humor that Finns can laugh about for hours, just remembering who the "big pant's" people were who got trapped in their humor. Such humor not only heats up a real Finnish sauna, but also brightens up the entire romp and frolic.

Non-communication among Finns is probably learned quite early on, since there are any number of things Finns don't talk about much. Personal body endowments or dimensions of either sex are never mentioned before, during, or after a sauna, except as a result of some crass invasion of upper-midwestern subculture. Finns never talk about their wealth or personal holdings, nor do they ever discuss their family or children. It seems it's bad luck to do that. It's just business, work, and enterprise they like talking about among themselves, and they do that endlessly.

The French, out there at the now defunct French Church on the West End, might have their elan residue; the Jewish community in town has its version of chutzpah, but none of these holds a candle to Finnish sisu. These Finnish people are survivors. "Other people quit before a Finn gets started," is what some Duluthians once overheard two Finns saying in private, which got around Duluth pretty fast back in 1939.

Why Finns generally choose not to speak up in public (too much or too often) is *not* because they don't have anything to say. Rather they say it all through work. In fact, Finnish can't be heard outside of work, because it's too subtle a language. If you're not working, Finnish goes right over your head. And, if by chance you don't understand work, then you won't hear a Finn speaking. By Finnish standards, you're probably not deeply enough into your work anyway, so the message would be lost on you.

Naturally, Finns talk all the time, so you mustn't presume they are shy or uncommunicative. They have a lot to say, but it's mostly said in private conversations. To really grasp their meaning, it helps to understand how Finns really do communicate.

Years back, out at the Duluth Winnipeg & Pacific Railroad, on the Bridges and Building gang, there was Finnish truck driver, Toivo Karvonnen, whose "go-by" name was Pikko. He was about as tall as he was broad, which puts everything close to five-foot-four. Pikko would drive a load of bridging planks to a site, like the Oneonta bridge, and just wait. If he had to wait longer than five seconds, he'd start hauling over those planks, those eighteen-foot, four-by-twelves, on his shoulders to where the crew was relaxing. He'd drop a plank so close to the soft-toed boots of the crew, they'd get the message right away, because they knew that where the next plank dropped would put an OSHA inspector into shock — it would drop right on the toes of that lazy crew chief, and never a word was said. That truck would be then be unloaded at Finnish pace. Fast!

That's how Finns are. Super action communicators! Communicate through work! It works best; the fewer words said, the better. So, if a Finn was going to speak, everybody had better be there and be listening; there had better be local TV and radio coverage for the homebound. And, people should come prepared to hear and hearken, because this was no small matter. This was probably going to be earthshaking, as it was in when those Finns were overheard back in 1939.

(By the way, Finns also communicate well through color and design. A cheerful Finnish-American farmstead or cabin, homestead or business, might have purple shutters, green window trim, and blue walls. Those Finns usually are able to anticipate art trends

Just Keep Going North..

decades before they reach the lower Scandinavians or appear in Euro-New York styles.)

Well, finally some high-placed Duluthians couldn't stand the suspense any longer. The Mayor sent his aide over to the Finnish consulate on 1st Street to find out if they knew what was going to be said. The consulate secretary listened to her question, but not for one moment did the secretary's fingers halt their high-speed movement across the computer keyboard; she nodded appropriately, licked and sealed two envelopes, and then pointed with her nose to the copy on the screen. Unfortunately, the aide couldn't read Finnish so she returned to the Mayor's office having done no more than try to memorize a twenty-six letter Finnish word, which turned out to be the name of a fish and potato soup.

The delegation from the downtown banks and brokerage houses had no more luck in finding out what "Finn to Speak" meant than the Downtown Development Association head, the director of the Chamber of Commerce, or the chief of the Duluth Tourist & Entertainment Bureau. It seems these groups chose to arrive during the busiest time of the day over at the Finnish consulate, which as every hardworking Finn knows, is sometime between 5:00 a.m. and sundown. The consulate officers were eager to help, but between answering phone calls, feeding the Fax machine, and filling out bilingual forms, it was all they could do to indicate with shrugs and impatient toe-tapping gestures that such information would be forthcoming as soon as the work was done.

Well, what that Finn was going to speak about was recognition well deserved. It seems the Finnish Government wanted to bestow some honors on persons of Finnish descent and merit. Two Duluthians who had shown some aptitude for the Finnish virtues of hard work and the ability to smile in adversity were made honorary Finns, with the right to walk in the annual St. Urho's Day Parade. And wouldn't you know it; those Jarvimaki brothers were also singled out for awards. The Jarvimaki brothers sure got what they deserved, as everybody in town knows full well.

They got the Suomi Order of the Roaring Lion, its fiery tongue cast forward in heraldic form, with its tail coyly lashing the waters of the Gulf of Finland. Yep, two Roaring Lions of Finland, Second Class, were awarded to those Jarvimaki's. Attired in the finest formal wear Duluth could provide, Waino Jarvimaki was inducted into the Mannerheim 2A Class, for Finnish-American persons "Distinguished in Business Acumen and Recovery." Vic Jarvimaki got the Mannerheim 2A Class for "Economic Assistance to the Finnish Brother & Sisterhood." And both brothers received a gold medal from the Finnish Heritage & Fraternal Life Insurance Association in Minnesota. Vic, who's the taller of the two, was too shy to say more than, "Thank you. Yep, that sure is nice," while Waino, beaming in his tuxedo, managed to add, "That sure is nice. Yep, thank you."

So now those Jarvimaki brothers have a titled lifetime claim to achievement. At the Duluth Zoo, where their rides have become a great hit, especially those old egg-shaped sauna units, they're addressed as Sir Waino Jarvimaki and Sir Vic Jarvimaki, which is better than they want, but not less than they deserve. And you can be sure they wear those medals, too, as a reminder to keep working.

(But matters didn't end there. The Swedish population in town as well as certain German and Norwegian segments — each having remnants of knightly orders back home in the old country — were obviously jealous over those Finnish honors and awards. Imagine, just imagine, giving Duluthians awards of nobility. So don't be surprised if you read that some Danish baker or a Swedish pulp cutter gets knighted or if a ladyship is bestowed on a some rosemauling painter from Duluth.)

Chapter sixteen

Now That's A Real Parade

The Duluth Parade of Homes has nothing to do with the activity backed by realtors and construction firms in other cities to showcase their new offerings or designs. It's strictly a Duluth venture, dating back to the now defunct Cotillion Club (which ran from about 1936 to 1958), to summer dances and member open houses, all the things that appeal to fourth-generation Duluthian East Enders who didn't benefit much from a liberal arts education. This Parade of Homes also appeals to newcomers, especially those eager to fit right in with the Duluth set.

The Parade idea is stimulated by the promise of a June that's been preceded by a not too rainy May, plus the slight hope that the iris and the peonies (the major perennials that thrive in Duluth) might just overlap in their blooming, that the winterkill condition of the lawn might recover just enough to match the newly patched driveway.

Actually, this whole Parade thing pretty much centers on the East End of town, with just a few select homes from the East Hillside and the West End participating. This has something to do with blatant geography and social class, with being in the right neighborhood, having solid Duluth property values, plus some real classy social contacts in Duluth. But, for many people for whom this is a Really Big Deal, the problem is getting over two big hurdles. The first hurdle is the Duluth Garden Society, and the second is the Duluth Junior League (or just Leaguers, as they prefer to be called).

The Garden Society consists of a loose bunch of bonafide "clumpers," persons who have earned the right to such exclusive club membership by earning fifty points for demonstrating their ability either to grow grass or a flowering outdoor plant. A perennial, such as lily of the valley, counts for one point, while something exotic, like a fringed geranium, is worth maybe two and a half points. It all depends on what the judges had for lunch. Then, too, the Garden Society is responsible for maintaining and policing small garden areas throughout the city.

Just Keep Going North..

So, the Garden Society selects the Parade homes on the basis of the artistry of the yard and garden, which is no small task since the judging takes place in early June. June is the time when Duluth yards and gardens have barely recovered from the ravages of winter, while the whimsy of summer is still ahead.

(Most tourists, and, of course, most Duluthians, don't know it, but the beautification of the city is a constant battle between the City Planning Department, the City Forester's Office, and the Garden Society. It seems the City Planning Department favors the natural northern look, which means wooden frames filled with bricks, crushed Duluth bluestone, and gravel beds, which all work together to create the distinct image of a building materials inventory lot or an artificially cratered surface from a distant planet. Offsetting these sterile designs is the business of the City Forester, whose job is to tear up those rock and gravel moonscapes and plant red maples and trees able to withstand tundra conditions. Sandwiched between these aesthetic giants is the Duluth Garden Society, whose efforts seemed to be trampled on by some "conglomerate urban vision" stemming from various eastern schools of landscape architecture, not to mention the limited growing season. As one Garden Society member related, "Here was this one city worker digging holes right in our dahlia beds on Grand Avenue, while the other worker would just fill them in afterwards. He'd dig a hole and the other worker would fill it in. I finally asked them what they were doing, right in our dahlia beds, digging holes and filling them in. And then that city worker came right out and said that the person who was supposed to plant the trees was sick that day. Imagine, putting trees in our dahlia beds! I couldn't believe it!")

The Junior League has a part in this Parade of Homes, too. Its understated role is to determine whether or not the aspirations, life-style, and status pretensions of potential applicants are worth reviewing at all.

Naturally, there is no snobbery in Duluth, especially among Junior League members; snobbery is alien to this association. Snobbery is what others use to fill up any deficiency in their virtues, their sense of community service, and the God-given ability to discern who has (and who lacks) enough quiet grace, wit, and charm to warrant undisputed membership in the Junior League. In Duluth, twenty percent of the standards that guide the Junior League are

Just Keep Going North..

carved in marble and stand on the edge of the Civic Square, much to the anguish of the ACLU, especially its former director. The remaining eighty percent of the criteria are known only to Junior League members, and it would be most unwise to rummage around in such matters, if not wholly indelicate.

So, the Parade of Homes centers on the East End of town. The fourteen homeowners selected each year spend three weeks getting ready for the big day. I leave it to your imagination to figure out how the Junior League committee members coordinate and interact with these lucky families selected for the Parade of Homes, because this is a test. Your imagination is either under control or it's running wild. If it's running wild, you could qualify for Junior League membership. It also helps to be blond, less than thirty-five years old, and droll.

The Parade of Homes homeowners are asked to demonstrate their right to enter Duluth's gentry and to be at least as creative as the Junior League sponsors, who are often quite eager to demonstrate real creativity in matters that should not concern us.

In more practical terms, this means the Parade of Homes homeowner should prepare a tour script for visitors, concoct something unique by way of an hors d'oeuvres sampler, and provide a small memento — even an item made by the householder to be given to visitors — preferably something under $1.75 per visitor in order to stay under the $8.75 Parade of Homes fee.

Naturally, there are certain social criteria the Parade of Homes householders must meet: single homeowners are excluded, unless they are over age fifty-eight and have with very high social class standing, plus a background in mining, timber, shipping, or tapdancing. Accordion players, transient academic types, and attorneys tend to have their gardens and life-styles disqualified rather quickly, but only on the basis of their occupation and landscaping concepts, not their otherwise amiable personalities.

In the Parade of Homes, each homeowner is asked to dress in attire that captures the period or style in which the home was built, which puts most things back to the 1890s - 1910s. Those quarter- to a half-million-dollar neo-ranch and "midwest modern" houses designed by eclectic and kindred Bauhaus architects using overworked Duluth bluestone as a prime building material, well, these homeowners could dress somewhat as they pleased, which usually resembles an overlay of country western atop a basic Levi and

Just Keep Going North..

Dock-schnocker ensemble. Then, too, some of these Parade homeowners choose attire to reflect interpretive home use, which pretty much has to with interior mood-management, which includes electronic gadgetry, lighting, and sound systems. These persons wear sterile-room attire and let you know that dust particles and smoke are anathema; they spend a great deal of time installing and checking out their air-filtration systems, especially for fog-laden micro-traces of sulfur by-products and heavy metals.

* * *

Janet Loffness, she's with the Duluth Tourist Bureau, learned from one of those down-state newspapers smuggled daily into Duluth that a group of Japanese businessmen were going to be in Duluth during the height of the summer season, right about the end of June. Of course, she'd never get such information in advance through the Northland print media or other sources. It seems these Japanese wanted both to scout out local business opportunities and property values and vacation. No slacker in following up such information, Ms. Loffness immediately phoned the Japanese consulate in Los Angeles and invited the visiting businesspersons to a "first-hand" exposure and "Discover Duluth" experience. You'll have to imagine for yourself how these curious Japanese reacted to this invitation, since the translation was sloppy. (As determined later, much to the deep embarrassment of all involved, it appeared Ms. Loffness had invited twenty-two Japanese businessmen to "Discover her talents and have a first-hand experience near the Head-O-The-Lakes.") The idea positively enthralled those Japanese businessmen, even to the point of foregoing their usual consensual decision-making. Hai!

Of course, true to her profession as a tourism promoter, Ms. Loffness arranged for twenty-two seats on the Twin City/Duluth regional bus (only to learn that Japanese prefer air travel over uninteresting surface travel). Janet also hired a Japanese student from U.M.-D. (only to discover that Japanese was her second language and that this young lady knew mostly Kobe slang, her father being a Japanese embassy official originally from Kobe, but now assigned consulate duties in Seattle). She even got the big newspaper in town and the *Grudgeteer* to promise to send out photographers to cover site visits and the Japanese visitors. Finally, something was going right

Just Keep Going North..

in the Duluth Tourist Bureau, or so it seemed on that foggy afternoon in June, and, it involved that Parade of Homes.

* * *

The idea of attending the Parade of Homes was really promoted by Louise Hoffman, the activity director out at the Grand Ave. Manor Sr. Citizen's Residence, all eleven stories, which makes it the tallest building on the West End. Well, if you knew Louise, you'd know she isn't the kind to just let those senior citizens vegetate, much less watch TV, or just sit and converse. She's a strong believer in activity, a lot of activity, for those Seniors, such as hikes up to Enger Tower, organized shopping tours to the mall, picnics down at Park Point, even winter outings and skating on Twin Ponds. Most of the senior residents tolerate Louise because once in a while she does come up with some entertaining events.

Like the time when Louise organized that taffy-making party that almost put Selma Kronstrom into cardiac arrest; that sly Hjalmar ("Hooty") Lindqvist managed to drape strings of gooey taffy all over her party apron, dress, and hair. Selma had visited the hair stylist that morning, and she was fit to be tied after that taffy party. Of course, that was real fun for some of those Seniors, at least some of the residents thought so.

It seems that Selma Kronstrom is kind of uppity at times and the news of the week going out by phone was what she did to that Hooty Lindqvist. She'd gone downtown and bought some rabbit food pellets, which she put on his medicine tray for a week. Strange, it seemed to cure his constipation, which led him to ask the visiting physician what that new medicine was. Naturally, that's when everyone learned about Selma's sense of humor, so now she's regarded as one of the crowd. The sons and daughters of the residents don't know quite what to make of all these strange goings-on out there at the Manor. It seems they're into more fun than senior citizens are rightly entitled to. Why, those Seniors are into comedy scripts that would put Hollywood to shame. Practical jokes are kid's stuff compared with what these folks do right under the nose of the administrator and staff. That's half the fun — getting something past Mrs. Virginia Leachman, the building director, and Louise, too.

Just Keep Going North..

Louise manufactures her own version of fun, which is a bit difficult for some of these older Head-O-The-Lakes types to grasp. It's a bit hard to get over being dour after a lifetime of practice; for some it's a bit strenuous to be outgoing with strangers, since they mostly want to be left alone to pursue their own ambitions. Having never in their lives had anybody direct their activities, you can't help but imagine their surprise when they're told there is a person *employed* just to put some continuous activity into their golden years. The reaction of some of these Seniors is predictable; they simply spend a lot of time tolerating Louise while they figure out another good comedy routine that mostly pits the older ladies against the older gents. They never volunteer any ideas to Louise, figuring that's what she's paid to do. It amounts to a cordial and pleasant "struggle for survival" between the activity director and the residents, which after all is one way to keep mentally alert.

Knowing that Ms. Hoffman was out to keep them busy, the best thing to do was to show her how busy they were with their own private agendas. However, Louise knew they were trying to avoid what was best for them. She'd remind them at breakfast of upcoming events for that day; she'd tweak their guilt feelings about not participating as much as they should, or even remind them they should get their dollar's worth of fun out of retirement home existence.

Ninety-eight-year-old Gladys Klingmann, an adherent of the Hoffman "go down swinging" theory for the elderly, usually added her two cent's worth by raising a liver-spotted hand and admonishing her junior residents to greater activity. "Get out there, pitch in, and do something," she'd say, hinting that she was going down to the Ten Cent Store at the West End to get some *Muscle-Beach* magazines, and did anybody want to join her?

So, Louise went from room to room signing up as many reluctant residents as she could find to attend the Parade of Homes on next Saturday. It took a real sales job on her part to get sixteen residents on her list. Frank Barnes, eighty-seven, thought the idea of going to a parade was OK. Yep, he'd go. He liked parades, although maybe Frank's hearing aid batteries didn't quite help him get the entire message. Emily Bergson said she'd go, if her friend, Enid Bachman, would go, but not if it was raining or if there was a televised Twin's game. And Inge Engebretson said she'd go, if her daughter didn't visit that day. It was tough saying "no" to Louise because she'd

Just Keep Going North..

just sit on the edge of a person's bed, with those piercing blue eyes, wringing her hands, until you said "yes."

On Saturday noon when the bus arrived, sixteen clearly dignified and obviously not overly eager senior citizens were lined up in the lobby waiting to get on with another Hoffman adventure.

"It's your last chance to use the facilities for awhile," said Louise, adding that some of the gentlemen might wish to take advantage of this opportunity. Glenn Erickson thought that might be a good idea, since things have been running close to a thirty-eight-minute cycle for him, what with his new medicine and that wristwatch reminder and all.

There's something uniquely refreshing about senior citizens all dressed up, something that has nothing to do with dress or style. It has to do with dignity and poise, with proper manners and courtesy. Of course these retired people wouldn't admit there was anything special about going to see another person's home. Why, they used to do that all the time in the old days. Maybe, these homes were different. Maybe they could discover what it was that made families so different these days, so unlike the family life they knew, and why their own children had such different values. Maybe these houses, built by people with a kind of success different from their own, would hold a message they hadn't heard before, a message they should hear, even if it was too late to do much about it. Maybe, these Homes-on-Parade had a sense of humor, a laughter spirit that only the elderly could hear.

In general, the fourteen Homes-on-Parade more or less fall within western culture as interpreted by Duluthians. Overall, I'd say their owner life-styles, gardens, and other status pretensions aren't too different, say, from what one finds in the Lake-o'-the Isles, in Minne'hapless, or along Summit Avenue, down there in St. Paul. Old is old, regardless of how it's sliced, and there are just so many things worth seeing in antiquated homes, restored or not, much less new homes on their way downhill, at least in Duluth. But some of those Home Paraders deserve mention, lest the rest of the story seem bland.

The fourth house site on the Parade of Homes was held in common by Tim Schmederhorn and Jim Plowder. Their house was in perfect order as a matter of inclination and practiced museum keeping. It all rested on their joint need for nest-building, which, in turn, was buttressed by their relational preference. There weren't any

Just Keep Going North..

children to consider, not with the French silk drapes, the Armstrength floor carpeting, and the solid walnut furnishings obtained from various house sales.

The facts about such homemakers — harder to garner in Duluth than elsewhere — are far more common than suspicions would indicate. After all, with all those big houses in Duluth awaiting restoration, persons of that persuasion tend to really get into repairing capital sinkholes. Who else in their right mind would sand, paint, restore, and otherwise pursue such activity as a life outlet, except slightly disoriented male bower birds?

So, if seeing some pretty good chintz covers over couches in a sunroom, sanded and urethaned floors, a restored 1932 Sears walnut dining room set and hutch, is what flaunting one's preference is all about, then the Schmederhorn/Plowder place is worth the visit. Reality testing is painful, but no less painful than parading the truth in Duluth.

The ninth home on the Parade of Homes was owned by Dr. Clinton and Amanathea Smith-Hameltopf; for Amanathea, Smith is a maiden name, and she's an artist. She does fantasy watercolors of plants and scenes that are supposed to symbolize the North Shore. Her artistry mostly resembles finger-paintings of pubescent seventh graders; these comparisons were made several times by the arts editor down at the *NooStribune*, much to the rancor and displeasure of Amanathea (that is, Amanathea Smith-Hodgegill, Radsteppes, 1974, $1, Hasty Tarts & Pussy Willows Society, B.A., French and Studio Arts).

Their home has been converted to a multi-tiered studio, from the basement to the attic. And the basement has been converted into a series of micro-surgical "operatories" so that Clinton can rehearse dramatic obstetric and gynecological scenes (complete with models and taped playback responses provided by interns). The main floor is restored as a New England uncomfortable area: a dining room, living room, and kitchen (no TV or other modern appliances worth noting), but equipped with sturdy Shaker replicas, including a wood-burning stove, an icebox, a real flour bin, and pantry. It's so quaint, you might wonder why they bother.

Of course, on the second and third floors, except for the children's quarters, the other four bedrooms and attic space are pure white-walled, northern exposure atelier, creative space for creative

Just Keep Going North..

finger-painting ala Northland scenes. The neighbors mentioned Amanathea finally managed to sell one of her paintings — aside from those donated to the St. Louis Co. Historic & Arts Center, down at the old converted railroad Depot — for about $45. It was a large one, too, about six-by-eight-feet, called "White-out with Birch Trees & Stuff."

Then there's Gin and Bruce Tomlasvessen's place. That's number five on the Parade. They've got a pretty good house, if you overlook the location. Their house sits right over the 3rd Street ravine and Congdon Creek, right out there in Crescent View. Yep, the creek meanders right beneath their house. It's a bit eery listening to those nearby storm sewers discharging into Congdon Creek, but it's probably worth the price of housing novelty in Duluth. This house was built by a theosophist back about 1907, and has a number of curious murals and symbols within its timbered and stuccoed interior. (Later owners didn't know what a theosophist was, so those murals and curious drawings were preserved out of sheer superstition.) As it turns out, the theosophists themselves don't know what the murals and symbols represent.

Gin and Bruce have made up a story about the building, which includes episodes about various next-door neighbors, wailing voices at noon, the possible spectral forms of Madame Blavatsky, Mrs. Beasant, and a series of "hidden masters," all of whose voices are heard giving messages regularly through the cold-air return and a 1928 Hoover vacuum cleaner in the hidden rearward chapel area of the house. If you happen to be in Duluth during the Parade of Homes, you sure don't want to miss the Tomlasvessen's place.

* * *

True to form, the Japanese businessmen arrived on schedule, deplaned, and assumed preplanned photographic positions on the tarmac, again at the airport entry, at the luggage station, and on leaving in their air-conditioned bus to Greater Duluth; the photo session was resumed at the Holidaze Inn, and at the restaurant for the noon meal, after which these stolid businessmen climbed aboard their bus for the survey and field tour around Duluth. The bus group leader/informant had a clipboard full of notes. Moving three miles-per-hour down Superior Street, the businessmen were apprised of the civic center, the Duluth Fun Center, the library (book capacity: 289,300 print), and a host of other quaint downtown features. The Japanese immediately commented among themselves on the curious arrangement of roadway bricks that made the street lanes zigzag along Superior Street. (It seems, perhaps, as if the roadway bricking was done before the sidewalk spacing was set, which goes a long way toward accounting for why the streets zigzag. Of course, the Japanese had another explanation.)

"Maybe too much sake," suggested one businessman.

"Ah, no," said another, "maybe labor problems and have to re-train workers on each block."

These explanations for the curious roadway pattern in downtown Duluth evoked such good humor among the businessmen that each tried to outdo the other; each sought to create a more entertaining answer. (Like Finns, Japanese have an awesome sense of humor, but it is confined to very private moments, as these businessmen experienced while driving in downtown Duluth.) The Japanese concluded that Duluth people, too, have a good sense of humor. The crazy lanes in the streets were a huge civic joke to inspire Zen koans. Why do roadway lanes change every block on Superior Street, in downtown Duluth? To make life's inconsistencies self-evident. Good thinking reduced to simple practice. Ah, indeed, these Duluthians might be much sharper than they appeared, the Japanese concluded. They weren't more than 180 degrees off the mark.

Naturally, the Japanese, the senior citizens, and other groups using bus service were scheduled to arrive at homes at about the same time. This was so the householders could handle the tours as large groups; single parties were urged to wait and join a group tour.

(Of course, everyone recognized the person from the City Assessor's Office trying to mingle with the crowd in order to discover taxable property improvements. The nun's disguise was ingenious, but flimsy.)

By the time the groups reached the sixth house in the Parade, Frank Barnes had seen enough homes for one day. He remarked to Louise Hoffman that this wasn't exactly the kind of parade he thought it was going to be.

"Some parade," he muttered loud enough for everyone around him to hear. "The houses stand still while the spectators have to walk around. Boy, things sure have changed from the old days."

Just Keep Going North..

Frank said he liked it better when those Shriners and the high school bands just marched by. "Whose idea of a parade is this, anyway?" he asked.

The wine coolers served at the sixth through the ninth houses rejuvenated Frank Barnes a bit. They didn't help Glenn Erickson at all, though they did loosen up Enid Bachman and Emily Bergson a tad. The Japanese were a bit suspicious of the fruity flavor, while most Duluthians recognized the distinctive white wine and seltzer recipe, complete with the pineapple and grapefruit mix.

Adhering to their customs, the Japanese (and a few other Paraders of Homes) took off their shoes and placed them in the entry areas. It made some of the householders a bit more comfortable seeing stockinged feet cross their Persian rugs and polished wood floors. But, then, wear and tear is part of the cost of opening one's home to the public, even on the outside. Visual wear and tear is what a lot of Duluth homes suffer from.

Emily Bergson had been diligently collecting those mementos, those remembrance souvenirs from each house she visited. Her oversized Mexican handbag was getting pretty full of those doodads. She thought it was a bit curious that so many of the homeowners had these small-sized men's shoes in the entry area. Mostly black-polished shoes. Maybe there was some significance to shoes this year that she didn't quite grasp. She made a restrained point of taking one or two shoes at each home in which they were displayed. Her oversized handbag now bulged with close to five odd shoes and two full pairs. Emily had even convinced Enid Bachman that they were supposed to take those shoes; after all, that's what they were there for. They were unusual souvenirs, but maybe that's why they called it a Parade.

Several Japanese businessmen were missing one or both shoes, not to mention a few other Paraders. Naturally, for the Japanese it would have been unthinkably impolite to ask such charming hosts what might have happened to their shoes. Perhaps it was an American custom to polish the guest's shoes on such visits. Or perhaps these Americans were examining the quality of their shoes, as one of the Japanese suggested to another.

"That old lady with the big flowers on her hat in the white dress is putting my shoe in her market bag. See, she is taking my shoe!" whispered Sato Ichihiro to one of his compatriots. "Look, but do not stare. Her woman-friend is doing the same thing. Is it not strange why old ladies would exhibit such behavior? I heard that many American women have a foot fetish, but I have never seen this before."

Surreptitiously, the two Japanese observed the two senior citizen ladies select and then stuff another shoe into each of their bags.

"Pahldone me, glacious senioh rady," said Mr. Ichihiro, "do you enjoy rearry good shoes? I could get you some reaarry fine ones, if you tell me why you co'lrect my shoe." Mr. Ichihiro smiled and bowed slightly, watching a surprised look appear on Enid's face.

"Oh, dear me," responded Enid, "this couldn't be your shoe. These are souvenirs. See, the homeowners have put them here as keepsakes to show that we visited and walked through their house. See, a shoe means to walk." She moved her hands in a shoe-like fashion to mimic traipsing through a house.

"Glacious rady," insisted Mr. Ichihiro, "I aszheuw you that is my shoe. See, my name inside it."

"Dear me, I'm afraid I can't read what it says," replied Enid, "but I'm sure this can't be your shoe. This is a gift from house number nine on the Parade. See, it has number nine right here."

"Crazy two old mama-san!" mumbled Ichihiro to himself in Japanese. "Those old women go around and steal men's shoes and enjoy themselves. Americans ought to take better care of their old women when they become dangerous to themselves and others." Ichihiro was unable to convince the rest of his friends that two old women had stolen his shoe.

"They'll probably return them at the end of the tour," counseled one of the senior Japanese businessmen, who had been to Detroit, even Washington, D.C. "It is probably some local custom we do not know about. We must not offend these Duluthians if we are going to buy businesses or property here. Just forget about it, Sato. Your shoes are not as important as good impressions with these unusual people who own this big lake."

"We think everyone should have a home as nice as ours," said Amanathea Smith-Hameltopf to all her guests as they left. "And we hope you'll all come down to the art fair at the Depot if you liked my impressions of the North Country," she added. Several apparent-

Just Keep Going North..

ly abandoned shoes on the floor caught her attention. Oh, my, she thought to herself, there are some extra shoes leftover. She raced to bring them out to the bus transporting the Japanese.

"You Duruth-Ame'ricans, have good sense of humor," said one of the Japanese businessmen. "We do not want to spoil your joke, so we wait to get the other shoe at end of trip, when all shoes reappear, polished and cleaned. Very good custom! VVVelly hospital people here in Duruth, even old radies who are tlained to take shoes when left unguarded," he said smiling, and added, "we have extla pair shoes in our ruggage bag here, not to worry."

"I haven't figured this all out," said Janet Loffness, grasping Amanathea's arm, "but I'm sure it's part of Japanese culture ... something about leaving a shoe on the property they hope to return to, like a penny thrown into a fountain."

"Of course, why, yes, I do remember something about that mentioned in Far Eastern studies, back at Radsteppes. What a silly goose I am; how could I have forgotten," she remarked, and laughed as she carried the shoes back to the house.

Glenn Erickson's watch reminded him every thirty-eight minutes that he had eight or less minutes to locate a toilet. That wasn't difficult. Except when he walked into the Tomlasvessen's living room, he felt that urge coming slightly ahead of time. Maybe it was the sound of water underfoot, maybe it was hearing the trickle of Congdon Creek as it spilled water lakeward. Regardless of the reason, he sure had to find a bathroom in a hurry.

Slightly embarrassed, he asked Gin Tomlasvessen where her facilities were located, and he was directed to the half bath near the entryway. His business was over shortly, but he couldn't open the door. Yup, it seemed stuck. Try as he could, the door wouldn't budge. He tried gently calling out, but no one answered. He tried shouting, but got no response. Surely, he'd hear the rest of the Paraders on their way back. So, Glenn just sat down and waited.

"Howjda' do," came a voice from the cold-air return. "You gonna' be here long or are you the new owner?" asked the voice.

"What's that? Whad'ja say? Where are you?" demanded Glenn.

Just Keep Going North..

"I'm here in the cold-air return. I live here, except when I take a fancy to the old Hoover vacuum cleaner in the back part of house," answered the voice.

"Oh, yea? Really! No kidding! And, what'cha do in the cold-air return?" asked Glenn, thinking somebody was having a little fun with him.

"Mostly, I just listen to old Crosby and Sinatra records, play solitaire, and tell stories to anybody who'll listen," responded the voice. "Wanna' hear some great World War II stories? Or, how about baseball? By any chance, do ya like baseball, like those Brooklyn Dodgers? And what ever happened to that Joe DiMaggio?"

Meanwhile, the rest of the gang had exited the house from the rear basement door to get a better view of the Congdon ravine and creek. Soon enough, Glenn's absence was noted.

"Where's Mr. Erickson?" asked Louise Hoffman. "Now, you folks just stay put and get back on the bus and sing some nice song until we find Mr. Erickson."

Well, finding Mr. Erickson wasn't a problem. Understanding what he was doing did take some getting used to, unless you think talking into a cold-air return is normal for Duluth. (Don't dismiss the idea out of hand.)

By this time, Glenn was down on his hands and knees talking through the grate of the cold-air return. Here was a somebody, a something, he could really talk to. This somebody made more sense than most of those old codgers that lounged in the TV common room back at the Manor.

"How'd you like to come out and live at the Grand Ave. Manor?" he asked. "Seems to me you wouldn't take up too much room, would hardly eat much food, and we could talk about the good old...."

At that point Louise Hoffman and Bruce Tomlasvessen managed to unstick the door and rushed into the room. Yep, there was Glenn talking a blue streak into that cold air-return, still on his hands and knees.

"I gotta' go now," said Glenn, "but you think about my proposition. I'll get back to ya, or you can just come on over if you want to. Don't pay no attention to this Ms. Hoffman; she's just paid

Just Keep Going North..

to keep us busy and active most of the time. Yes sirree, we could really talk about the old times."

"C'mon, now, Mr. Erickson, we mustn't keep our friends waiting out on the bus," admonished Louise. "And, besides, you really don't think there's anybody down there, do you?" she asked patiently.

How Louise managed to trip over that old Hoover vacuum cleaner as she backed out from the bathroom area was certainly curious. Neither Gin or Bruce Tomlasvessen had any idea how that vacuum cleaner had gotten there. Anyway, it seems Louise's dignity was injured more than her sense of purpose.

It was a tired but satisfied group of Seniors that returned to the Grand Ave. Manor Sr. Citizen's Residence. Glenn had almost convinced Frank Barnes that he was going to have a roommate pretty soon, and that he'd met this nice old gent living in a cold-air return. Of course, Glenn more properly suggested that "this person" was only living in a basement and needed more fresh air.

"You can be sure that Erickson's up to some more of his tricks," remarked Inge Engebretson, adding, "I'll just bet he doesn't think we know about ventriloquists. He just did that voice thing to scare Louise. I heard her say she was going to call Glenn's son and tell him that maybe his father was getting a bit senile, and they'd have to keep closer tabs on him."

If Glenn was pulling the activity director's leg, if he was up to one of his tricks, we'll never know. But, it seems he's a lot happier now that he's got a person he can talk to, a real live-in friend out there at the Manor.

* * *

For the Japanese, it was a different matter. They squirmed around a bit before finally, but politely, inquiring about their shoes. They thought it was time for the joke to end.

"Shoes? What shoes?" asked Janet Loffness, astonished by such a question.

"The shoes those two old ladies take to enjoy, to polish and shine, and return. Enough good humor. Where are our shoes?" demanded the Japanese leader, bowing slightly.

Janet was dumbfounded. This wasn't what she'd learned in tourism courses. What could these people possibly mean, she wondered.

Finally, one of the younger Japanese screwed up enough courage to ask: "Ah, so, Missa Roffness, maybe you take our shoes until we poritely ask you the right question. OK, baby, I ask you: how you wanna 'discover the big Duruth' with me? OK, then we get our shoes and go. OK, how about that 'first-hand experience,' you leady? OK? Youll place or that nice hotel down the sleet?"

I guess those Japanese discovered a kind of Duluth that far exceeded their expectations, if Janet's talents and first-hand reactions were correctly reported in the *NooStribune* the next day. This misunderstanding caused considerable embarrassment all-around at first, what with those businessmen expecting more than the Duluth Tourist Bureau could ever deliver. And, of course, the missing shoes added to their consternation, but they knew when they'd lost the battle.

Clearly, the Japanese felt Janet had "out-faced" them, "out-qualit-ied" them in good humor, and, with a perfect straight-faced response, outwitted them. What a woman! Such an assured samurai tactic. What a perfect Zen solution: innocence is bliss; absolute innocence is absolutely confounding! They concluded they wanted to look more deeply into Duluth, maybe even to the point of building a pasta-noodle factory, maybe a shoe factory, or even buying a few old houses. Duluth could be converted into Ginza II, if they could convince Janet to serve as their director-organizer. And with those crooked lanes in downtown Duluth, bad luck could never follow them more than one block at a time. It was a city made for Japanese acquisition, a block at a time.

* * *

Emily Bergson felt obliged to write thank-you notes to all the Parade of Homes homeowners. She'd read in the *NooStribune* about two women who had been seen stealing shoes. Together, she and Enid Bachman had about six pairs of black shoes, plus eight or so odds and ends. She indicated she was distressed about the matter and would bring those shoes right out on the bus. She was so embarrassed, so upset, so distressed. She'd never done anything like this in her entire life before, and she hoped the homeowners wouldn't be unforgiving.

Emily feared senility like sin. When she'd discovered those shoes weren't souvenirs, she just sat on her bed thinking to herself. Oh, Emily, you're not with it any more. You're losing it. Oh, Emily, what would Harold say if he were alive and here?

She actually felt better that Harold wasn't around. He'd just say something like "My God, Emily, where is your mind, girl? What could you have been thinking about? This is like the time you spilled ten pounds of sugar during food rationing ... or the time you washed my real silk tie. But then I've been saying that for thirty-eight years."

Emily completely forgot about the matter when Hooty Lindqvist knocked and peeked in her room and said, "Hey, sweet thing, whad'ja say you and me hike down and get some lunch. I hear Louise Hoffman's resigned and we're gonna' have a big send-off party soon."

Well, parades come and go, which is natural. You could hardly expect them to stand still. Yet, life in Duluth is hardly a spectator sport, as it is in other places; it's more like seeing what wasn't supposed to march by or walking forward just to keep abreast of the parade.

The neighbors think the Parade of Homes misses the point. The point is: you'd better get your own cold-air return and start talking because pretty soon nobody that counts will be listening to you, anyway. It's all going to be watching and programmed activities. It's all going to be taken for granted. And going to somebody else's house had better not be to discover what's different, but to discover a laughter spirit that's worth hearing and taking back with you. That's the real meaning.

ABOUT THE AUTHOR . . .

RICK EICHERT was born and raised near the edge of Lake Superior. Until he left Duluth to earn the highest academic degrees available from the "Big U" down in "Minn-hapless," he had been told there were no known life forms south of Hinckley, Minnesota. Educated and self-taught in both the Liberal and Conservative Arts, Eichert passed the time in teaching, tweaking fellow-educators, and later embarked on a career in industry. Naturally, the gravitational pull from Duluth was too great to withstand. Eichert returned to Duluth in 1973, where he mostly spends his time collecting and cleaning local foibles, reading "Letters to the Editor" in the *NooStribune*, and writing never-mailed sarcastic rejoinders, all of which provide the basis for these tales about the North Country. Intrigued by the complexity of life manufactured locally in Duluth, and given his extensive commercial and published products history, Eichert used regional English and idioms to weave these improbable stories from the flim-flam, and the jetsam and flotsam, that collects daily at the Head-O-The Lakes. No small task!

Though basically shy, Eichert has won several literary awards and has an extensive publication record in the social and behavioral sciences; he has national stature as an educational materials designer, and is otherwise able to produce evidence of a regular means of livelihood, the latter being necessary to avoid possible vagrancy charges in Duluth.

JUST KEEP GOING NORTH ... YOU'LL KNOW WHEN YOU GET THERE!

Imagine what would happen if you cut off the tip of the largest of the Great Lakes, put 85,000 plus dour Scandinavians, Germans, and twenty-five other ethnic groups together on shore, added the fun and games of industry and city government, and then threw in a culture based on tourism, taconite, and just plain tom-foolery. Why, you'd have Duluth! You'd have an endless source of mishaps, planned and accidental, worth relating. You'd meet the Jarvimaki brothers and their Fast-Track Sauna & Sunshine Clinic. You'd learn why household water service is regulated on odd and even hours of the day, and how important skipping stones and calming the waters are to the locals. And, if you ever wanted to know where the real action is in the North Country in a real town, *Just Keep Going North ... You'll Know When You Get There!"*, is your road-map to adventure with unpardonable, but sturdy, characters from Duluth.